Dr Krissie Ivings is a Consultant Cl
and Hypnotherapist, whose do
relationship between beliefs abou
giving up. She set up and ran NH   , smoking groups and
workshops, with a remarkable 70% success rate. As a former
smoker herself, she is passionately committed to helping other
people to discover the freedom and joy of no longer having any
need or desire for nicotine in any form.

First published as Free Yourself From Smoking in Great Britain
in 2006 by Kyle Cathie Limited, 122 Arlington Road London NW1
7HP

ISBN (10-digit) 1 85626 657 5

ISBN (13-digit) 978 1 85626 657 4

Cartoons brought to life by Paul Fitzgerald of polyp.org.uk

2nd Edition Published in Great Britain in 2025 by
Printexpress (Buxton) Ltd.
The Old Schoolhouse, Market Street, Buxton SK17 6LD

ISBN: 978-1-7395903-3-8

Contents

Acknowledgements

It is strange to be back in the world of smoking cessation after almost 20 years. And there are 3 main people responsible for the resurrection of this part of my life. The first is Mark Davis from The UK College of Hypnosis and Hypnotherapy. He invited me to take part in a webinar on why a Consultant Clinical Psychologist with 25 years' experience had decided to learn about clinical hypnotherapy. During that webinar he grilled me at length on smoking cessation and rekindled my curiosity about issues I spent years working within, but had then left behind completely.

Mark has also been extremely generous with his advice on the hypnotherapy scripts, about which he knows far, far more than me. Many of them are adapted from his own, or lifted in their entirety from him.

The 2nd pair this book owes its life to are my twin daughters Katie and Isobel, who – despite having been successfully steered away from cigarettes - took up vaping in their later teenage years. Thus becoming one of many millions of young people hooked on vapes in a world-wide epidemic that INFURIATES me, as it simply never needed to have happened. (More, MUCH more on this in the pages ahead). Both have now quit – thankfully – and their insights into the minds of vapers were invaluable. Particular thanks to Isobel Ivings who copy edited this book, as well as contributing significantly to the vaping intel.

I'd also like to thank Ryan Sherwood, of Printexpress Buxton, for patiently putting up with my 11 'final versions'.

Preface: who I am and how to use this book

I am a Consultant Chartered Clinical Psychologist and Clinical Hypnotherapist. I did my doctorate on smoking cessation, and I set up and ran very effective and popular groups for the NHS based on what I discovered in my research, which explored people's positive beliefs about smoking, and the extent to which people could change how they think and feel about cigarettes.

As a former smoker, I became fascinated by the psychology of smoking. When I looked at the research evidence, and the literature on smoking, I discovered that most advice focused on the following things:

- Help to deal directly with the withdrawal symptoms by using patches or other products containing nicotine

- Strategies to help people change their behaviour

- Health education

- Motivational support

What appeared to be missing were ways to help people fundamentally change the way they think about their own smoking or vaping, and their positive view of cigarettes/e-cigarettes.

The academic literature is full of direct experimental evidence that shows that smoking does not relax people, but rather that smokers are more stressed than non-smokers. It even shows that when people stop smoking their stress levels drop, and continue to drop for as long as they remain non-smokers. The psychological literature recognises that smokers are often illogical or irrational, and it also stresses the importance of helping smokers change these irrational and inaccurate beliefs if they are going to quit successfully.

More recent research on vaping shows exactly the same patterns: which makes sense as vaping is really just a different way of getting nicotine.

But despite these insights, when I spoke to practitioners in the field of smoking, they tended to be pessimistic about the chances of changing a belief such as 'smoking relaxes me'. Even more importantly, some professionals I spoke to did not view statements like 'smoking relaxes me' or 'I enjoy a cigarette' as merely a belief that might or might not be accurate, but as a statement of fact. They did not seem to understand nicotine addiction any better than their clients did.

The treatments most commonly offered to smokers do not directly address a crucial part of the Nicotine Addiction Triangle: distorted positive beliefs about smoking.

In other words, although psychologists had recognised the importance of thoughts, attitudes and beliefs about smoking for a long time, this knowledge was not really being used to help smokers quit.

My doctoral research

I therefore decided to research the positive beliefs smokers have about their smoking more fully. [1]

The research questions I was trying to answer were:

- Do smokers have strong positive beliefs about smoking?

The answer was yes. (No surprises there!)

- Can these beliefs be changed?

The answer to this was also yes. This was exciting confirmation that smokers really can learn to think and feel differently about their smoking. This was extremely important since many people, including those working in the field of smoking cessation, do not recognise that a lot of what people say about their own smoking is distorted. Of course, I am not saying that smokers are telling fibs - but they are making mistakes. They do not truly understand their own smoking, so the reasons they think they smoke are not accurate.

The obvious next question in my research was:

- Does changing their beliefs help people stop smoking?

This time the answer was yes - up to a point. In my research I directly compared 2 different treatments. The first treatment was delivered by therapists trained by Easyway's Allen Carr, who kindly cooperated with this research. They focused on changing beliefs about smoking and nicotine addiction.

The 2nd treatment was delivered by an NHS based smoking cessation service, which focused on behaviour change, education, motivation and nicotine replacement products.

Both approaches worked about as well as each other. Since people did change their beliefs about smoking in the Easyway group, but only about 30% of them stopped smoking, clearly changing beliefs alone was not enough.

I then developed a new approach that combined different aspects of the smoking trap. When I evaluated this combined approach, I was excited to see that it was more effective in helping people stop smoking than either approach offered alone – almost doubling the quit rate of the other 2 separate treatments.

Since then, I have also trained in hypnotherapy, which is likely to add even more effectiveness to the approach, as hypnotherapy is a powerful tool for fostering lasting changes in thoughts, feelings and behaviours.

The approach can be summarised in what I call the Nicotine Addiction Triangle, which addresses the three factors of physical addiction, psychological dependence and habit.

Addressing all angles of the Nicotine Addition Triangle is much more useful than focusing on just one or two pieces of the puzzle.

My approach has been evaluated according to the Department of Health's own strict guidelines and published in a peer reviewed journal. [2] It has been proven to be extremely effective. This book therefore gives you the best possible chance of freeing yourself from smoking, vaping or any other form of nicotine addiction permanently.

How to use this book

As we will learn, understanding how nicotine addiction works is far more important than relying on willpower when trying to quit. This book explains why most models of smoking or vaping are wrong or incomplete. It teaches a new model (the Nicotine Addiction Triangle), which explains why people smoke or vape, and why stopping feels difficult. Once you understand these concepts you can stop more easily, and permanently.

These insights are supported by 8 relaxation, meditation and self-hypnosis downloads that help with every aspect of preparing to quit, quitting and staying quit for life. The downloads are just 5-20 minutes long, which means you can listen to them regularly, and play them whenever you feel you need a boost.

Each chapter introduces a new idea or set of ideas that help you to build up a complete picture of your own smoking or vaping.

Each chapter finishes with a summary of the key points, which you can return to after you have finished the book to remind you of the main issues.

The book includes worksheets and behavioural experiments to support your own exploration and understanding of smoking and vaping. Behavioural experiments are incredibly valuable information gathering exercises, designed to test the accuracy of an individual's beliefs, or to test new, more realistic and helpful beliefs. I don't want you to take what I say on trust - I want you to *know* these truths for yourself, and to fix the truth about smoking firmly in your mind.

The book teaches you how to stay stopped, and what to do if you are struggling, including downloads to maintain your commitment to your goal, and to manage high risk situations after quitting.

After we have built up a complete understanding of nicotine dependency, and helped you apply it to your own situation, you come to the main event - how to quit. Please don't turn straight to the 'How to Quit' chapter. You will get there soon enough. You cannot put those chapters into practice until you have built the foundations, and prepared yourself for possible pitfalls.

Relaxation, meditation and hypnotherapy downloads are used throughout the book to help you make an emphatic and determined decision to quit happily and confidently.

The 4 relaxation and meditation recordings can be used anytime. However, the 4 hypnosis scripts need to be played at the right times as you go through the book. They won't make sense if you have not read the chapters they relate to. There are also some hypnosis scripts that are specifically to be used on quit date and would be far less effective if listened to before you are ready to benefit from them. The self-hypnosis chapter explains exactly how and when to use each recording.

The book addresses all forms of nicotine addiction, including addiction to nicotine gum or other Nicotine Replacement Therapies. Where relevant, I address different forms of nicotine intake separately, but for most of the book the issues are identical, no matter how you get your nicotine. I use the words smoke or vape interchangeably at times, and the word 'smoking' refers to both cigarettes and e-cigarettes.

Downloading the Recordings

The following link takes you to the section of my website from which you can access all the recordings.:

www.aspirelifestyle.co.uk/scripts

Then enter the following code:

DitchNitch

Chapter 1:
Why Does Quitting
Seem So Difficult?

'It's easy to quit smoking - I've done it a hundred times!'

MARK TWAIN

Quitting smoking is a phrase that strikes fear into the hearts of most smokers. The difficulties of quitting are legendary. Almost all smokers have tried to stop, and many have tried dozens and dozens of times. In my treatment groups a number of people always said despairingly, 'I've tried everything - from acupuncture or hypnotherapy to patches, gums and sprays to sheer willpower or out and out bribery. Nothing works!'

Even those who haven't personally suffered have no doubt heard plenty of horror stories about the difficulties. I heard them myself week after week at the start of Stop Smoking groups. As people were waiting for everyone to arrive they chat to each other. It made depressing listening:

- 'A friend of mine whose son is a heroin addict says that quitting nicotine is harder than stopping heroin.'

- 'Something like 95% of people fail apparently.'

- 'My wife says she'll leave me if I don't quit but I still don't think I can.'

- 'My doctor says I'll lose the leg unless I stop so now I really have to quit. But then I've been saying that for years.'

We have all heard stories of people continuing to smoke after their legs have been removed, or after heart attacks or surgery for lung cancer. Most of us have met people who quit years ago and still declare that 'not a day goes by when I couldn't murder a cigarette'. This sends a desperately pessimistic message to people who want to stop, making them think, 'If it's really that hard and it never gets any easier, how on earth am I going to do it?'

Other people talk about addiction as an incurable illness. The illness can be controlled but never erased - once a smoker, always a smoker. Yet others view addiction as a character flaw suffered by those with an 'addictive personality'. These widespread beliefs are also shattering to the motivation and self-esteem of a smoker. If it is impossible ever to be truly free of smoking, is it worth making the effort to quit? The message appears to be crystal clear: Giving up smoking is incredibly difficult. Most people fail. You yourself may have failed on previous attempts. If you try to quit, you have a very good chance of failing again.

Vaping is a more recent problem, but the issues are identical – for the simple reason that vaping is just another way of getting nicotine. Some methods of quitting that rely on grim facts and figures about smoking to scare people into stopping, work even less well for vaping, as the health risks, while considerable, are not as bad as those for smoking. Luckily my approach is not fear based, but focuses on freedom. Which means you can quit e-cigs just as easily as you can cigarettes.

However, with these beliefs so common it is no wonder so many smokers choose to ignore their fears about smoking and keep their heads firmly buried in the sand. If they are condemned to lifelong smoking, why torture themselves with all the possible consequences?

Fortunately, it does not have to be this way. But it is important to understand the problems if you are going to avoid them. So even if you find the descriptions of quitting depressing, don't be afraid to keep reading.

Why does stopping seem so hard? Why do people feel they cannot stop? To understand the reasons for such high failure rates, even among people who are desperate to quit, it is necessary to· explore the quitting process in detail. Like most things in life there are many ways to go about it. Unfortunately, in the case of ending your relationship with nicotine, most people choose to go about it the hard way. This is called 'white knuckle quitting' - it even *sounds* hard.

White knuckle quitting

By far the most common method of quitting is using sheer willpower. If you calculate the costs of smoking and compare them with the benefits, the answer is obvious: the costs outweigh the benefits, so you should quit. Unfortunately, knowing that smoking and vaping are really bad for your health and wallet makes no difference to how much you want a cigarette or vape. In fact the more scared you are of being dependent on a harmful drug, the more you feel you need that hit, because nicotine calms you down!

Think of it as a seesaw. At one end is the desperation to quit and at the other end is the desire to continue. Your mind seesaws back and forth between smoking/vaping and stopping. Scared of carrying on but even more scared of life without your faithful friend.

A quit attempt is triggered when the balance tips just far enough towards the stopping end of the seesaw. Perhaps you develop a cough. Perhaps your children ask you to stop. Maybe money is a bit short at the moment, or you notice you can no longer walk up the stairs without wheezing. Or perhaps that social event where you need to repeatedly go outside in the rain for a puff becomes utterly tiresome. Maybe you are zero-ing a vape in an airport toilet before a long-haul flight, feeling humiliated and ashamed, and think 'enough!'

You make the decision to stop and almost immediately doubts and fears creep in. Before their attempt, people try to bolster their willpower by marshalling all these excellent reasons and fixing them firmly in their mind. This is a good way of enhancing motivation - after all there are hundreds of excellent reasons for stopping.

Some people write out the stark statistics about smoking to try to scare themselves into stopping. Or read up on the chemicals, carcinogens and heavy metals in e-cigarette aerosols. This can work quite well initially. While people are still smoking, the reasons for stopping are in the forefront of their minds. Fear, anxiety, guilt or shame are triggered every time you puff, thus increasing the desire to stop. Many people manage to stop for a while using this method.

Others make deals or bargains with themselves or other people. This can feel quite motivating and provides good incentives to keep going with the quit attempt.

These approaches help you to focus on stopping, and can be helpful - up to a point. The problem is none of them make any difference to how much you want to keep smoking. Wanting to stop doesn't stop you wanting to carry on. Both can easily be true at the same time.

Key Concept

> Wanting to stop does not stop you wanting to carry on! No matter how excellent your reasons for stopping are, they don't stop you wanting the next hit.

This is why people think willpower is so important. It feels as if the only way to quit is not to let yourself smoke or vape, even though you desperately want to. That quitting involves gritting your teeth and toughing it out. So, with your long list of reasons to stop smoking, you flex your willpower muscles, firm up your resolve, and recite the reasons for quitting to yourself over and over again like a mantra. And then, with a sense of anxiety and loss, you take your last drag and wait for the torture to start...

Many quit attempts never get beyond the first day. The minute you finish the final puff, you want another one. One woman in my group described what happened when she last tried to quit: 'I threw away all my cigarettes, determined that I would do it this time. Ten minutes later I was on my hands and knees fishing them out of the bin again.'

Some people last longer than a day. Some even last a few weeks. At the beginning of a quit attempt the reasons for stopping may be enough to overcome your on-going desire to continue. But what happens as time goes by?

Well, the obvious change is that you aren't vaping or smoking any more. This means your fear and anxiety about it are reduced. The pressure has eased and is no longer at the forefront of your mind. But your desire for that nicotine hit does not diminish. You want a puff as much as ever. In fact, you often want it more than ever because your memories take on a rosy glow that bear little resemblance to the reality of life as a nicotine addict.

Gradually, fear of smoking or vaping stops being able to outweigh the desire to have that hit, and your thinking about smoking and vaping changes totally. Instead of focusing on the negative aspects, you are now consumed with thoughts of what you are missing out on.

As a quit attempt progresses, fears of smoking fade, while your desire for that relief stays the same or increases. This is why reasons for quitting, such as health and cost, are seldom enough to stop you permanently.

Once you are in that sort of state of mind you will be looking for a way out. A get-out clause that lets you have a sneaky puff and makes that decision seem okay to you. And we are all very good at coming up with those...

Pick a reason, any reason...

- It's clearly not the right time for me.

- I'm too stressed at the moment.

- Things are too bad at work.

- My family need me to be supportive; they shouldn't be expected to put up with this.

- It's selfish of me to continue when it's affecting me so badly.

- I owe it to my boss to smoke again so I can function properly.

- Life's too short – might as well enjoy it!

- They say everything gives you cancer anyway.

- Just one won't hurt.

The balance tips towards the re-starting end of the seesaw and with a sense of relief and release you light up - Aaaahhhhhh that's better! How did you ever imagine life without that wonderful feeling?

Why does it go wrong?

When people try white knuckle quitting, the initial motivation to stop can be very powerful. Some admirable people actually do struggle through the misery of the first few days and weeks hoping that one day the cravings will go away. But they don't. In fact they sometimes get worse. No matter how determined that person was to start with, the motivation to keep on with the quit attempt seems to fade while the urge for nicotine is as powerful if not more powerful than ever. So why does this happen?

When a quit attempt was first triggered, all the reasons for stopping were hitting you in the face all day every day. The wheezing, the doctor's lecturing, the expense, the cough, the self-contempt, the children's anxieties, the tensions with your non-smoking partner, the hassle of going outside in the rain, the guilt, the fear of 'forever' etc etc etc.

When you stop, those reasons no longer affect you directly. The disadvantages of smoking change from being on-going stressful experiences to mere memories. And memories simply do not have the impact of real experiences. So the motivation for quitting begins to slide a little bit as the misery of smoking fades into memory.

But what about the advantages of the smoking end of the seesaw? That hasn't changed! In fact, the pleasures and benefits get elevated higher than when you were actually smoking. Recent ex-smokers put smoking high on a pedestal. They remember all the 'best' cigarettes and vapes, and think wistfully of all those wonderful smokes in lovely places, erasing the thousands of forgettable puffs, or the uncomfortable cigarettes in inconvenient places.

People start making random associations between smoking and good times. If they see a smiling smoker they think, 'That guy is smiling because he is smoking!' So, while the costs are fading, the benefits are becoming hugely exaggerated, with the result that the seesaw tips back towards smoking and the quit attempt fails.

Key Concept

People who quit nicotine put vapes/cigarettes on a pedestal. They then crave something that is better than the real thing!

Whatever your smoking history and whatever the costs of smoking are to you, the balance almost always tips back towards smoking in the end. Older smokers often think younger smokers could stop easily because they are not so severely addicted. On the other hand, younger smokers firmly believe that they would never let themselves smoke or vape for that long, or let themselves get to the stage of ill health and disability before quitting. The truth is that all smokers are caught in a similar trap. Whether you are younger or older, smoke just a couple a day or get through 1000 puffs daily, you are all stuck in the Nicotine Addiction Triangle, and will all experience similar problems in quitting.

The basic problem is that the misery of quitting seems directly proportional to the misery of smoking and so you stay in the trap. If you decide to quit because you tell yourself that you'd quite like to stop smoking, you can let yourself off the hook by telling yourself you'd quite like to start again now. Whereas if you tell yourself you absolutely have to stop because it is killing you, you also feel that you can't live without it. The more desperate you are to stop, the more desperate you are to continue. So no matter how bad smoking gets, the fear of stopping is as great or greater than the fear of continuing. People sense that they are stuck, and that they can't escape. It feels like the ultimate Catch-22. But don't panic! This book will explain why that happens and show you how to overcome the problem.

Key Concept

> Your desperation to stop is balanced by your desire to continue. So the more you want to stop, the harder stopping feels.

It is important to recognise that our thoughts actually change when we start to smoke again.

Thoughts such as:

- 'I'm scared of getting ill' suddenly change to 'We all die some time'.

- I want to get fitter' becomes 'I can take up sport even if I smoke - balance is the key'.

- 'Smoking is a horrible habit' changes to 'Smoking is intensely pleasurable'.

- 'I'm sick of being a slave to a drug' becomes 'Cigarettes are always there for me, they never let me down'.

- 'It's embarrassing and anti-social when I have to go outside and puff' is now seen as 'Social situations are difficult without smoking' or 'Smokers are more interesting people'.

Once your own mind has started rebelling against your self-imposed deprivation you are on your way to smoking again. As you may well know from your own experiences, as soon as you are back on the slippery slope, your attempt to quit is doomed. One or two on a Saturday night becomes eight or ten on Friday and Saturday nights. Then you start smoking whenever you are out, so Wednesdays become smoking days too. Then you start going out more than ever before to give yourself an excuse to smoke. Then you start buying them again because your friends have got sick of you scrounging all the time. Before you know it you are back to the same levels of intake as before, and feeling more depressed and hopeless than ever.

Fear of smoking versus fear of stopping...

A huge problem with quitting is that smokers feel that there are basically only two options. And neither is attractive. First, you can stay as you are and keep on smoking. This is, of course, an expensive and unhealthy option but you won't be any worse off than you are now.

Smokers are good at hiding things from themselves. They are masters at the art of sticking their head in the sand and ignoring the grim realities of living (and dying) a smoker. Many smokers smoke for years on end and the thought of quitting never enters their heads. They simply feel that the misery of stopping would be unbearable, so they dismiss that option. They then have to try as hard as possible to ignore the misery of continuing and just try to make a virtue out of the necessity of keeping on puffing.

These are the 'die-hard' smokers who almost make a career out of their smoking. They believe that smokers are more interesting, that the best conversations at parties are outside where all the smokers are, that quitting is for holier-than-thou prigs or health freaks and that smoking truly and deeply enhances their lives. They often wear their ill health (such as a gravelly voice) like a badge of honour. They learn to blow elaborate smoke rings, do tricks with Zippos or buy custom vapes. They tell jokes like 'I never get sick - no germs could survive in my body.' Or they go to Vaper Expos, extoll the virtues of the DOJO Blast 6000 and write blogs on ever more ingenious ways to strengthen a vape.

Much as they might protest to the contrary, these people are just as keen to stop as every other smoker, and if a magic pill came onto the market that cured nicotine addiction immediately they would jump at it. In fact they do jump at it. Every so often a 'cure' for smoking is launched. It happened in the early 2000s with Zyban (Bupropion). It is the confirmed smokers who are first in line for those sorts of treatments. These smokers' basic problem is that while they long to be free as much as everyone else, they believe it is impossible without some 'magic' to take away their desire to smoke.

The second option is quitting. For those who do summon up the courage to try, the quitting option leads to real fear as the person imagines a future of endless deprivation and misery. Never enjoying a cup of coffee, or a meal, or an evening out again. Never having the ability to reduce stress. Never being able to cope. As John Reid, then UK Secretary of State for Health, remarked in early 2004, some people even feel that smoking is one of their few pleasures. With such strong beliefs about the attractions of smoking it is no wonder that quitting seems a pretty unappealing option too, but at least you would save money and make significant health and fitness gains.

Unfortunately, anyone who tries to quit is likely to enter the attempt with the real fear that they might fail. This fear is a powerful barrier to any serious attempt to stop. Even friends and family grow weary of the oft-heard phrase 'I'm going to quit' and respond with scepticism, if not outright derision. If no one else believes you can do it, it doesn't do much for your own confidence.

Being a smoker is bad enough at the best of times, but when people are smoking freely without thinking about quitting, they often manage to keep their head in the sand and ignore some of the risks and costs associated with it. A quit attempt involves taking their head out of the sand and admitting that they hate being a smoker, that they are terrified of the implications of smoking, and they are utterly sick and tired of needing to smoke no matter how inconvenient.

Taking a long, hard, honest look at your smoking and the effect it has on your life is fine if you then go on to quit. But what if you can't? What if you make these frightening admissions about how much you hate smoking, only to end up smoking again anyway?

But don't despair!

Now that I have thoroughly depressed you, I can assure you that it doesn't have to be this way. There is another way - to quit and be delighted to be shot of cigarettes or vapes, to feel free, and never to miss it at all. This may sound like an impossible dream, but it is possible and is already a wonderful reality for many ex-addicts.

This book will show you how to:

- Quit without misery and fear.

- Never miss cigarettes.

- Take cravings in your stride.

- Feel totally confident in your ability to succeed.

- Experience less stress and misery.

- Quit with a feeling of relief and freedom rather than anxiety or dread.

Despite the fact that many people find it hard to stay stopped, many others do succeed permanently and live perfectly happily without wanting or missing cigarettes or vapes. Many of you may have experienced this happy state in the past.

Often people who have failed in a quit attempt are doubly disappointed because they actually didn't find it that hard to stop. But for some weird reason, even though they stopped before and it was quite easy, they can't do so again now. Or people who just decide to stop, and do so with few problems, are pleasantly surprised but a bit puzzled at their success.

In my groups at least half the people say they have stopped for months or even years in the past and had no problems with stopping. But they started again for one reason or another and now have no idea how they ever managed without cigarettes. Even these people view being happy as a non-smoker as an impossible dream - although they themselves have been happy as non-smokers in the past. This is a good example of how the addiction affects thinking and reasoning. When you are addicted, being free of the addiction seems impossible. Yet as soon as you are free, you can't imagine ever getting hooked again.

In fact, we have all been happy to be non-smokers in the past - before we started smoking. Wouldn't it be nice if you could get back to the happy innocence of not being remotely bothered by cigarettes? Well, you can. That is precisely what you can achieve with this book.

Key Concept

No matter what your smoking history, you can be completely free.

It is perfectly possible to be permanently and totally free, no matter how badly you are addicted at the moment. But it is virtually impossible to control nicotine intake, no matter how easy it was to quit. In practical terms this means:

- Yes, you can quit!

- No, you can't have the odd puff now and again!

Where so many smokers go wrong is that they believe the opposite statements to be true. When they are smoking, they tell themselves they can't stop (not true!). But when they have stopped, they tell themselves they are safe to puff occasionally without getting hooked again (also not true).

Those lucky people who stop without feeling miserable have stumbled accidentally on a frame of mind that allows them to quit. But they don't understand how they got there. They don't know why they have succeeded in stopping smoking this time. So if they get caught by smoking again, they don't have the knowledge they need to escape.

Don't worry if you are not one of those people who have stopped without too much difficulty in the past. In my groups many people say that they have stopped before but found it a horrible miserable experience which was much too hard to sustain. These people can also stop easily and permanently. Others have never stopped for even a day before. They can also quit. So whatever your smoking and quitting history, you too can succeed in your dream of being totally free of all desire to smoke.

The aim of this book is to teach you the secrets of successful quitting. The key to successful and permanent quitting is to understand nicotine addiction.

Key Concept

Smokers do not need to be superhuman to quit! Understanding smoking is more important than willpower.

Chapter summary

- 'Everyone knows' how hard it is to quit. They are wrong.

- Most people quit using sheer willpower, or 'white knuckle quitting'.

- This is indeed very hard ...

- Understanding smoking is more important than willpower.

Worksheet

Getting started!

The first step to the new smoke-free you is to understand your own smoking. Fill in this table with everything good about cigarettes or e-cigs that you can think of. What do think you get from smoking?

What I Believe Smoking Does for Me!

Chapter 2:
Vaping, a problem that never needed to happen

Vaping is a public health catastrophe inflicted on us for absolutely no good reason at all. There was no need for vaping ever to have become the monster it is today. I truly believe vaping will be the next huge public health scandal as the true mental, physical and psychological impact on millions of children and young people slowly emerges in the years ahead.

And none of this had to happen.

I remember when I first heard about vaping. From the very beginning it was clear that there were 2 competing narratives at play. First, the obvious reality that vaping was being aggressively marketed to children. Alternatively, the naïve (or wilfully cynical) view of the government, and various public health bodies, that vaping was a useful aid to quitting, with no wider health risks.

I clearly remember literally shouting at the television as another government suit trotted out the absurd lines of 'there is no evidence that anyone takes up vaping, the only vapers are people switching from smoking'. I was shouting NOT YET!!! Because it was clear by then that vaping was being marketed as a sexy, exciting, new option for people, and particularly children, with flavours like bubble-gum, blue raspberry, candy floss etc.

The simple fact is that vapes already existed. They were called inhalators and were part of the existing Nicotine Replacement Therapy (NRT) range. They were sold in chemists alongside the Complan and the Preparation H. Not surprisingly, kids weren't overly keen, and indeed the only people taking up NRT were, and are, smokers trying to quit.

It would have been so easy to insist that vapes could only be sold in 3 flavours (tobacco, menthol or neutral), packaged in plain boxes and sold in chemists. If that had been done, vaping would have remained a smoking substitute option, of zero interest to non-smokers, let alone children. Do you know *anyone* who has never smoked or vaped who is addicted to nicotine gum or patches? Thought not.

But vaping was being aggressively marketed in a different way: sold in Head Shops, with funky flavours on the high street. And kids flocked to them in their millions: In 2023, 25% of 11-15 year olds had vaped in the previous 12 months. [1] In the USA in 2018, 30% of under 14s had vaped. That number is almost certainly much higher now. [2]

There are additional problems with vapes. Cigarettes, for all their faults, are at least disgusting. So younger children generally all hate smoking and can't understand why anyone ever does it. It takes peer pressure in later childhood for most kids to be willing to start experimenting. Not so with vapes. They smell sweet and appealing so there is no in-built disgust. Studies in the USA have shown that children as young as 7 vape. [2]

Also vaping feels less grim than smoking. All kids hate their first cigs. Not so vapes, which means it is possible to vape more frequently, and take in much more nicotine than you can when you first start smoking.

It seems clear that the removal of some of the built in physiological limits to how many cigarettes you can smoke before throwing up means people can take in far more nicotine with vapes, developing levels of consumption that take the most hardened smokers decades to get up to. This can be the equivalent of multiple packs of cigarettes per day if people buy higher strength liquids, which are readily available, despite being illegal. Anecdotally it is not unusual to treat smokers who try to quit with vapes, fail, and – on returning to cigarettes - find themselves on 40 a day, not the 20 they were on when they started vaping.

Professor Blaha of John Hopkins University writes: "many e-cigarette users get even more nicotine than they would from a combustible tobacco product: Users can buy extra-strength cartridges, which have a higher concentration of nicotine, or increase the e-cigarette's voltage to get a greater hit of the substance."

This has created a perfect storm in which younger and younger children are taking in more and more nicotine at a stage where their brains are extremely immature. Nicotine changes the brain. We are setting these kids up for serious long-term and brain-based issues.

Nicotine adversely affects brain regions that control learning, mood, attention, and impulse control. This affects concentration, attention, focus and impulsivity. These changes are likely to be particularly problematic for children when their brains are still developing: missed learning opportunities in childhood cannot be recovered. [3] But it's not just kids who should worry – vaping damages adult brains too.

A 2022 Lancet Public Health review concluded that nicotine exposure in adolescence is associated with lasting changes in brain structure and function, impaired executive control, and increased vulnerability to mood disorders, addiction, and other substance use later in life. These harms are not limited to youth - research indicates that vaping can impair cognitive function and mood regulation in adults too. [4]

There is a lot of research connecting nicotine use to 'social maladaptation' – thoughts and behavioural patterns that make it more difficult for young people to navigate daily life. [4,5]

Children who are vaping may be using nicotine as an artificial crutch far earlier than smokers, before they have developed skills in resilience, problem solving, peer relationships, and other developmental skills, which develop throughout childhood, and are crucial for skilful functioning in adult life.

Finally, research suggests a link between vaping and poor mental health, including anxiety disorders, depressive symptoms, and suicidal ideation. [3]

During the explosion in child vaping rates there has been a parallel rise in youth anxiety, depression, and self-harm, [4] and of ADHD and other neurodevelopmental diagnoses. [6] UK data show a clear upward trend in ADHD diagnoses among children and adolescents over the past 15 years with the proportion of 10–18-year-olds with a recorded ADHD diagnosis more than doubling between 2010 & 2018. This partially reflects greater recognition but also a genuine increase in incidence. Although comprehensive data beyond 2018 are still emerging, these figures point to a sustained growth in ADHD prevalence among UK under-18s into the early 2020s.

Correlation does not equal causation and increases in ADHD recognition from 2010 to 2015 predates the vaping explosion, so there are clearly multiple factors relating to this increase. Not least social media usage and pandemic related disruptions to schooling and social opportunities. However, a link with vaping is entirely plausible given the known effects of vaping on the developing brain, yet no large scale epidemiological studies have been done to examine this as yet.

The good news is that quitting vaping is almost exactly the same as quitting traditional cigarettes – and both can be easy if you know how. Nicotine is nicotine, and e-cigarettes work the same way as traditional cigarettes do. The advice in this book applies equally to vapes. Throughout the book, you can view the word 'cigarettes' as referring to e-cigarettes or vapes, as well as traditional cigarettes.

Chapter 3: Why Do People Smoke or Vape?

Smoking is full of paradoxes and contradictions. Until you can understand the following things, you will not be truly free:

- Nicotine addiction is vague, subtle and often barely noticeable **AND** nicotine addiction is a tremendously powerful force.

- You don't truly enjoy smoking **AND** smoking feels extremely enjoyable at times.

- Smoking/vaping reduces your anxiety **AND** makes you anxious.

- Nicotine withdrawal only takes a few days **AND** cravings can hit you months or years after stopping.

- You can get hooked on something you loathe doing.

Most importantly, you need to understand all aspects of the Nicotine Addiction Triangle. You need to know how your mind works against you in order to keep you smoking, or to make you start again if you have stopped. And you need to understand why the drive to smoke does not respond to logical reasoning - which is why you cannot talk yourself out of wanting to smoke.

In most quit attempts people think about all the reasons for stopping and don't pay too much attention to reasons for carrying on. After all, the pleasures and benefits of smoking are obvious... Aren't they?

Actually, no. The question of why people smoke or vape in the face of appalling costs is not immediately obvious. Yes, it's an addiction, but that is a description, not an explanation. Most people do not truly understand their own reasons for smoking and are not very good at explaining smoking.

Various psychological theories have been put forward over the years to try to explain smoking. But they don't answer the question very well either.

An example is the 'three-stage model' which claims that people smoke as a result of the interaction between three factors. The first is called 'psychosocial reinforcement' which covers things like peer pressure or the desire to be sociable. For example, smoking at a party when someone offers you a cigarette in order to break the ice, or to be friendly. The second factor is 'positive reinforcement' and refers to getting pleasures or benefits from smoking, such as improved mood, better concentration or relaxation.

The final factor is 'negative reinforcement', which means doing something in order to avoid or remove something unpleasant. For example, smoking removes withdrawal symptoms.

In other words, this model suggests that people smoke because other people they know are doing it, because they get pleasures and benefits from it and because if they don't do it unpleasant things happen. Sounds reasonable? Perhaps it seems to make sense because this is a description of virtually any behaviour - going for a jog, eating a chocolate bar, having sex, going to work. Most rational behaviours are influenced by what that behaviour can help you get - and by what it can help you avoid.

There is an inaccurate assumption among health professionals and smokers themselves that whether or not a person smokes is governed by the same sort of rational decision-making as any other behaviour. This view suggests that smokers weigh up the pros and cons and make a choice about whether to smoke. The researcher who developed the three-stage model wrote: 'Decisions are based ultimately on the subjectively perceived balance of advantages and disadvantages of smoking ... the decision is always a rational one from the subject's viewpoint.'

This sort of theory is not good at explaining addictions. (And if you smoke or vape, I can assure you that you are addicted to nicotine.) The assumption that smoking feels rational, even to smokers themselves, simply does not tie in with the actual experience of being in an addiction trap. One heroin addict wrote:

Hunting for a reason to stop that outweighs the drive to stay hooked is the major problem. During one soul-searching session I neatly listed advantages and disadvantages of taking smack. Potential consequences of using heroin included being charged with an offence, starring in a scandal, losing home, job, wealth, friends and credibility of every kind.

Advantages were impossible to find. The following statements appeared on the list of reasons not to stop: 'It [heroin] makes life easier'; 'I'm scared to stop' and 'I don't feel like it'. A moment's thought contradicted the first two and left me confronted by the third. I did not 'feel like it'. I did not stop. [1]

Nicotine is not heroin, but they are both highly addictive. While there are many differences between smoking and illegal drug use, the addictive processes behind all drug use are the same. As this passage highlights, no matter what they are addicted to, the addiction makes people behave in ways that are not rational - and they know it.

The actual experience of addiction is effectively captured by C. S. Lewis, who wrote of 'an ever-increasing craving for an ever-diminishing pleasure'.[2] This is a much better description of how it feels to be desperate to smoke cigarettes or puff on a vape that you don't even really enjoy, or want to do.

Key Concept

You can crave something you don't even enjoy.

Smokers are addicts. And they behave in ways that are not rational. This means that rational 'reasons' for smoking may not be the real reasons that people smoke.

The Nicotine Addiction Triangle

This book describes a different model of smoking from the 'three stages' mentioned above. I call it the Nicotine Addiction Triangle.

It is explained fully later, but in summary it represents three separate problems that smokers must overcome in order to free themselves from smoking or vaping.

1) Physical addiction

   Cigarettes and e-cigs are addictive, so part of the problem is that you need nicotine to feel okay. You feel anxious or edgy without it.

2) Psychological dependence

   You have strong positive beliefs about smoking that make the prospect of quitting seem scary and miserable.

3) Habit

   You tend to puff in the same places and at the same times, and those situations feel weird and difficult if you don't smoke.

What reasons do people give for why they smoke?

Why do people smoke? On the face of it, it seems a bizarre thing to do. Research has shown that most smokers and over 80% of adult vapers want to quit. Many make quit attempts every year. [3]

Despite declining smoker numbers, smoking remains widely recognised as Britain's biggest preventable killer - killing 72,500 to 82,500 people every year. Smoking is also ruinously expensive with a packet of 20 averaging over £15 a packet, equivalent to over £5000 every year if you smoke 20 a day.

Vaping is less harmful than smoking, but long-term data is not yet available and there are already known impacts on lungs & heart health, and on mental health, cognition and learning. Several serious or life-threatening lung diseases can occur, including sudden lung collapse and other diseases that can develop rapidly in young people. [4]

In addition, aerosols are known to contain:

- **Acrolein:** a cause of permanent lung damage, this herbicide is usually used to kill weeds.

- **Benzene:** a highly flammable chemical more commonly found in car exhausts.

- **Carcinogens:** chemicals proven to cause cancer, like formaldehyde and acetaldehyde.

- **Propylene glycol:** a synthetic food additive also used to make paint solvent and antifreeze.

- **Diacetyl:** associated with so-called 'popcorn lung'. Diacetyl is no longer permitted in UK vapes, but elsewhere vape liquids can still contain it.

- **Fatty acids** in the liquid that coat the inside of the lungs, and can lead to Lipoid Pneumonia.

Vaping is less expensive than smoking, but vapers can still easily puff through an elf bar a day at a cost of £5 every day – adding up to thousands of pounds per year.

Also, nicotine is a sympathomimetic drug. These are drugs that stimulate the sympathetic nervous system – our 'fight and flight' system. Nicotine increases cardiac sympathetic nerve activity, causing a pattern of heart rate variability which is associated with increased cardiac risk. And which directly increases anxiety through activating your fight/flight alert system. This happens no matter how you choose to get your nicotine. [5]

Both smokers and vapers suffer the enormous hassle of a lifetime spent feeding the addiction: Office workers and people out socially are forced to go outside to puff regardless of bad weather, running out is a major headache, scrabbling together enough cash can be a nightmare, as is having to go out at night to buy what you need.

These costs have not stopped you from smoking. Fearing the consequences is not enough to stop you doing it. Ironically, the more scared you are, the more you feel you need a nicotine hit! The problem is that you are smoking or vaping for a reason. After all, you aren't stupid or mad. If you are putting up with all this to smoke, you must be getting something in return. Cigarettes seem to be able to do things for you that you can't get from anything else. Everyone has their own reasons, but most people have at least some of the following beliefs about smoking.

Relaxation and stress reduction

Smoking is relaxing and relieves stress. Smoking helps you cope with life's difficulties. Smoking gives you courage and confidence to tackle difficult situations. In times of stress cigarettes or vapes are always there for you - endlessly reliable, ever dependable.

Imagine taking an exam or driving test. The cigarette does its magic before the test to help you cope with your nerves. After the test, they are there again ready to help you unwind. Or imagine being stuck on a delayed flight, stacked above Heathrow for hours waiting to land. Finally, your plane is diverted to Geneva where you face a night on a bench in the airport. There's little information and no compensation. You are cold, tired, frustrated and angry. But at least there is a smoking area where you can light up. Hurrah! You take a deep drag right down to your toes and feel the stress ebbing away instantly. Bliss! Can you imagine coping without it?

Concentration

Smoking sharpens you up. Smoking helps you to focus. Smoking gets your brain in gear. Think of the cliche of the overworked writer - cig in one hand, bottle of Jack Daniels in the other. When I was a smoker and I had a problem at work, a cigarette always seemed to help me sort it out. I could have a smoke and think the problem through. The smoke somehow seemed to help me think more clearly so I would find a solution. Smoking gives you that extra edge of creativity. Think of having to make a difficult phone call. A cigarette in hand gives you extra confidence to succeed. On long car journeys, cigarettes can keep you alert and focused. You have to make an important presentation and are up late working on it - cigarettes help you to stay sharp. How could you cope with the demands of a stressful life without cigarettes to give you a helping hand?

Enjoyment

'A woman is only a woman, but a good cigar is a smoke,' said Rudyard Kipling. Smoking and vaping are immeasurably pleasurable, and gratifyingly satisfying.

The taste, smell, sensation of inhaling and even the way the smoke curls seductively up into the air are all deeply satisfying pleasures. Merely the sight of a shiny new packet or bar can lift your spirits. Unwrapping the cellophane, extracting the cigarette, the sharp flare of the match or the satisfying click of the Zippo. The puff, the taste. All aspects of the experience are enjoyable.

Making good times better

No activities are complete without a smoke to go with them. No meal out would give pleasure if you couldn't smoke afterwards. A coffee without a ciggy or a glass of wine without an elf bar is like strawberries without cream. Can you imagine beers or cocktails on a lovely holiday evening without a cigarette or vape to go with them? Life without smoking would be duller and drearier.

Addiction

Quitting creates terrible withdrawal symptoms. If you stop, you'll climb the walls with cravings. You will be tense, irritable and thoroughly miserable. Your misery affects everyone around you, making them pray that you'll start smoking again because you are so unbearable to live with. Would your relationships even survive a quit attempt? And anyway, once an addict always an addict. You might quit for years and years but never a day will go by when you won't feel that you could murder a cigarette. Is it really worth all this misery?

In summary, smoking and vaping make good times better, bad times less bad, improve your concentration, are deeply enjoyable and satisfying, help relax you and help you cope with the stresses and strains of life. No wonder you don't want to give all that up.

At this point you may be suspecting that I am actually a pro-smoking, pro-vaping plant! I appear to be trying to persuade you how fantastic smoking is. If smoking really does all the above and more, then no wonder you smoke. And no wonder you are scared of stopping. If this were all true, the puzzle would be not that so many people smoke, but that **anyone ever manages to give it up at all.**

However, the truth, as you may be suspecting, is not so simple ...

Frankly, if cigarettes did all that for me, I'd still be smoking too. However, even though you might guess (quite rightly) that there is more to these 'benefits' than meets the eye, it is very, very important that you fully understand what you think you get from a cigarette or a vape before you try to quit.

Use the following questionnaire to try and get a sense of your own beliefs about smoking or vaping.

Beliefs About Smoking or Vaping Questionnaire.

TICK ALL THE STATEMENTS THAT YOU AGREE WITH IN THE FOLLOWING QUESTIONNAIRE.

☐ Cigarettes or vapes taste nice.

☐ Not smoking or vaping is uncomfortable.

☐ Smokers put cigarettes or vapes in their mouths without noticing.

☐ Being without cigarettes or vapes is very unpleasant.

☐ Cigarettes or vapes ease social situations.

☐ Puffing helps people forget their worries.

☐ Puffing prevents people slowing down.

☐ Handling cigarettes or vapes is part of the enjoyment of smoking.

☐ Some people smoke or vape for taste alone.

☐ Being without cigarettes or vapes is almost unbearable.

☐ People smoke or vape automatically without being aware of it.

☐ Smoking or vaping helps at parties if you don't know

anyone there.

☐   Smoking or vaping helps ease embarrassment.

☐   It looks good to be smoking or vaping.

☐   Smoking or vaping are sociable.

☐   Smoking or vaping gives you something to do with your mouth.

☐   Smoking or vaping helps people be more at ease with other people.

☐   Smoking or vaping are pleasant and relaxing.

☐   Quitting creates a really gnawing hunger.

☐   Smoking or vaping are stimulating and perk people up.

☐   Smoking or vaping helps people be one of the crowd.

☐   Life is easier if you can smoke or vape.

Add any others you can think of. It is essential you truly understand why you want to carry on. Why giving up feels scary. What you think your faithful friends offer you and your life. Without that insight, it is these reasons that will drag you back in the end.

And once you are clear in your own mind about the pleasures and benefits of smoking, consider the following question:

What about if those reasons are not actually real, but merely smoke and mirror illusions?

> **Key Concept**
>
> The reasons people think they smoke are the same reasons that lead them to relapse.
>
> Do not just try and scare yourself into quitting by thinking of the costs of smoking. Focus on what you get from smoking too.

- 'Reasons' for smoking make you too scared to even try to stop.

- 'Reasons' for smoking make success less likely if you do summon enough courage to try.

- 'Reasons' for smoking make your quit attempt feel miserable.

- 'Reasons' for smoking make it more likely that you will eventually go back to smoking if you do stop.

What a tragedy it would be if these 'reasons' were in fact false and flawed when they are so important in condemning you to lifelong smoking. You owe it to yourself to explore them.

Chapter summary

- 'Commonsense' models of smoking are wrong.

- Smokers have many reasons for smoking.

- These reasons make stopping seem difficult.

- Understanding your own reasons for smoking is essential if you are to be truly free.

Chapter 4:
A New Understanding
of Smoking

Meet Nitch

Now that I have just about convinced you that smoking is a great and wonderful thing to do despite its unfortunate costly side effects, I am going to state categorically that all the above is not true. Smoking and vaping do not give you any of the benefits or pleasures I have just described. In fact, they **do not achieve anything worthwhile for you at all.**

I know this sounds a bit much to accept - after all, you actually experience the pleasures and benefits that I am claiming do not exist. So on the one hand I am agreeing that you may indeed experience smokes as relaxing, confidence-enhancing, concentration-boosting, stress-relieving and enjoyable, but so that these pleasures and benefits don't exist.

In other words: You smoke. You enjoy it. It helps you feel & cope better.

But smoking is neither enjoyable nor helpful.

Huh?

Be patient, it will all become clear. One secret of successful quitting is to sort out this apparent paradox - to understand how the nicotine addiction triangle tricks you into believing smokes and vapes help you, when in fact all the benefits are costs in disguise.

Key Concept

'Benefits' of smoking or vaping are really costs in disguise.

To understand how thoroughly you can be fooled into believing the myths about cigarettes you need to meet a little creature called Nitch. Nitch stands for Nicotine Itch, and Itch stands for:

Irritating, Time consuming, Controlling and Horrible

Introducing Nitch

Meet Nitch. He's a little parasite who lives inside you. He feeds on nicotine. When he has nicotine, he is as quiet as a little mouse. When he is deprived of nicotine, he winds you up and stresses you out. In terms of not taking no for an answer, Nitch is in a league of his own. Nitch needs nicotine to live. Without a regular supply he will die. He depends on you to keep him supplied. He needs to make certain that his supplier (i.e. you) continues to feed him no matter how expensive or inconvenient that may be, and no matter what the health cost to you.

Nitch doesn't care if the nearest cigarettes are in the twenty-four-hour garage ten miles away and it's blowing a blizzard outside.

It's nothing to him if getting a packet of cigs or a vape means not being able to afford food. So how does he manage to make assertive and independent people quite such slaves to his desires?

Everyone who smokes or vapes has Nitch inside them. You too have a Nitch that lives in you.

Nitch has two weapons: anxiety and propaganda.

Anxiety

When people smoke, the following cycle occurs over and over again.

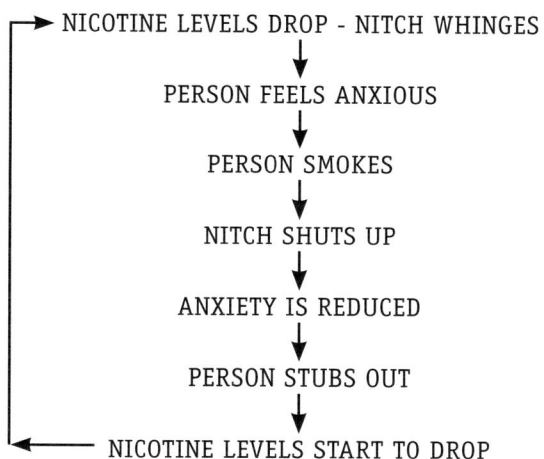

```
    ┌──► NICOTINE LEVELS DROP - NITCH WHINGES
    │              │
    │              ▼
    │       PERSON FEELS ANXIOUS
    │              │
    │              ▼
    │         PERSON SMOKES
    │              │
    │              ▼
    │        NITCH SHUTS UP
    │              │
    │              ▼
    │       ANXIETY IS REDUCED
    │              │
    │              ▼
    │        PERSON STUBS OUT
    │              │
    │              ▼
    └──── NICOTINE LEVELS START TO DROP
```

This process is also shown in the following diagram.

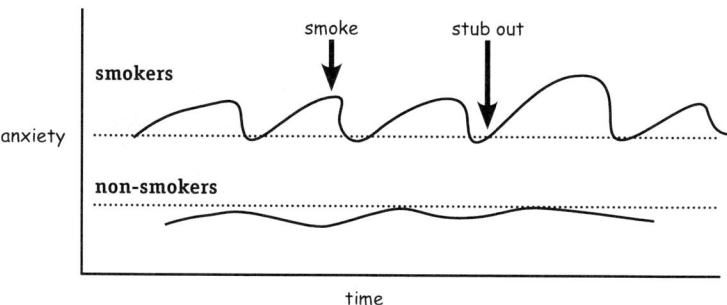

Nitch makes a fuss as soon as the nicotine levels in your blood drop. He makes himself a nuisance by making you feel tense or anxious. When you smoke, the feeling vanishes instantly, so the cigarette is experienced as relaxing and relieving. But by smoking you guarantee that the tension and anxiety return as soon as Nitch feels hungry again.

This feeling of anxiety is caused by nicotine withdrawal: it is an artificial, chemically induced anxiety. But it feels no less real for that. We are all powerfully motivated to reduce anxiety, because anxiety is a danger signal. Our unconscious mind thinks that when we experience anxiety it is because there is some danger around, and it prompts us to do whatever it takes to reduce the anxiety. This strong unconscious drive to reduce anxiety has nothing to do with how unpleasant anxiety itself is - early flickerings of anxiety are not painful. The strong drive to reduce anxiety is a survival mechanism because our unconscious mind thinks that anxiety = danger, and it wants us to get away from the danger.

Usually, this mechanism works just fine. If we stand too near a cliff edge, we feel a little anxious, so we move back a few steps. This is helpful behaviour. It goes wrong when the anxiety is caused not by danger, but by the chemical reactions triggered in nicotine withdrawal. In this case, the drive to reduce the anxiety, with whatever it takes, leads us to make a mistake. We learn very quickly that smoking reduces this anxiety. So we smoke. This is not a rational attempt to make ourselves feel better, but a biologically driven attempt to reduce anxiety, (and therefore make us more likely to survive).

After we stub out a cigarette Nitch is only quiet for a few minutes. Then, slowly but surely, he starts whining again. Smokers are so used to this that they barely know Nitch is there. He has them so well trained that he just has to give a little peep and they obligingly light up again, sometimes without even noticing they are doing it.

In my groups some smokers always say that they don't know why they smoke most of the cigarettes they smoke, as they 'get nothing from them'. In fact, they do get something from them - a bit more peace from Nitch. It's just that if they respond to Nitch quickly, before he gets into a real strop, they barely notice the difference when they shut him up.

In psychological terms this process is called negative reinforcement. A reinforcer is something that increases the likelihood of a behaviour being repeated. Positive reinforcement means increasing the likelihood of the behaviour by giving something desirable when the behaviour occurs. For example, eating chocolate is positively reinforced because it tastes delicious. Negative reinforcement means increasing the likelihood of a behaviour because the behaviour removes something undesirable, such as anxiety.

Anything we do that reduces anxiety is reinforced, so we are more likely to do it again. In smoking, the anxiety is chemically induced. There is no real danger. But the survival mechanism is not sophisticated enough to tell the difference between anxiety born of real danger and anxiety created by nicotine withdrawal.

This is the first angle in the Nicotine Addiction Triangle: the physical drive to smoke, arising from physical addiction.

Key Concept

We are programmed to reduce anxiety by whatever means possible. This is a biological survival mechanism.

Let's think again about Nitch. Whenever he makes a fuss, and you feed him, you are rewarded. So your smoking behaviour is reinforced repeatedly, hundreds of times a week. If you try to limit your smoking Nitch gets more and more upset with you, and makes more and more of a fuss. When you do finally give in, you reduce more anxiety, and the relief feels tremendous. This is why some cigarettes are experienced as amazingly wonderful, while others aren't that big a deal. When we are smoking freely, we barely notice the anxiety. But when we limit smoking there is a greater amount of anxiety when we do finally smoke, so the cigarette is experienced as more satisfying.

The most 'enjoyable' cigarettes or e-cigs are generally the ones after a period without smoking, for example straight after getting off a flight, after a meal, or when we get in from work. These cigarettes are simply the ones that end a bigger Nitch tantrum. The illusion is that they are 'better' than the ones we chain-smoke. But the reality is that Nitch made us more anxious before the 'best' cigarettes, so we experienced greater relief when we shut him up. This is the same process that makes food taste so much better when we are hungry - the hungrier we are, the more rewarding eating is.

The anxiety caused by Nitch builds up gradually over time. It is also vague, subtle and no different from the general anxieties of life. So smokers don't recognise that Nitch is making them anxious. Their impression is that they feel a bit better whenever they smoke. The true situation is that smokers are almost permanently stressed by Nitch, and what feels 'better' is simply the temporary removal of this chemically induced state of anxiety.

It has been known for a long time that smokers are more stressed than non-smokers. People used to believe that this was because people who had more stressful lives tended to smoke. In fact, research has now shown that even if you take all other factors into account, smokers are still more stressed and unhappy than non-smokers. When people stop smoking their stress levels begin to drop, and they carry on dropping for as long as they stay off the cigarettes. People who start smoking again only show rises in stress levels *after* starting again, which proves that they do not simply start smoking again because they are stressed.

In addition, smokers are much more likely to develop stress-related disorders such as agoraphobia, panic disorder and generalised anxiety disorder than non-smokers.

It is quite clear that far from helping you deal with stress, cigarettes actually cause anxiety. And no wonder! Having Nitch living in you, giving you hassle whenever he gets a little low on nicotine, is incredibly stressful. It's like carrying around a permanent parasite you can never get rid of, even for a few hours. Nitch will never learn any manners or patience, and will never go away. He doesn't understand the words 'no' or 'later'. He is as persistently irritating as a toddler in the chocolate aisle of a supermarket.

And he gradually gets stronger and stronger as his need for nicotine increases.

Smoking is no more than an attempt to be free of Nitch's whining. Smokers spend their lives trying to rid themselves of the aggravation of this little pest. But by smoking they are merely keeping him alive and well, ready to irritate and distract them some more, soon after stubbing out.

Key Concept

Nitch causes anxiety. Smoking appears to be helpful because smoking shuts Nitch up for a while. But it also keeps him alive, so that he can stress you out again.

So how does he get away with it? Nitch's power is in the timing of the anxiety. When people think about their own smoking, they generally focus on what is happening just before lighting up or actually during smoking.

But you are a smoker twenty-four hours a day, so it is just as legitimate to look at a different part of the cycle. Let's start with stubbing out or putting down your vape. After you take your last puff, you have enough nicotine to keep you feeling fine for a while, but your blood nicotine levels start dropping and you gradually enter a period of nicotine withdrawal. This causes anxiety. When you smoke again, Nitch shuts up and the anxiety vanishes. This relief is almost instant, and it is perfectly obvious that it is the puff that has made you feel better. On the other hand, the smoking-related anxiety builds up gradually, and so the smoker does not link it with nicotine withdrawal, and with the last cigarette they had. So cigarettes get all the credit for calming you down but none of the blame for stressing you out.

The feeling of wanting to smoke is an entirely artificial feeling that was created when you got hooked on smoking. The stress of needing to smoke is caused by nothing other than smoking.

Key Concept

Cigarettes/e-cigs get all the credit for calming you down, but none of the blame for stressing you out in the first place.

People view smoking as a welcome pleasure in a stressful world. Giving up is seen as the loss of something truly precious. The reality is that Nitch is an unwanted intruder in your life, who creates anxiety, and never leaves you alone. Quitting simply means freeing yourself from the misery of life with Nitch.

Propaganda

Nitch's ability to stress you out through blood nicotine levels is, however, only one weapon in his armoury. Even more powerful is his phenomenally successful use of propaganda.

People will believe virtually anything positive about smoking. They will also disbelieve virtually anything negative. How and why this bias in our thinking arises is crucial in understanding the secrets of successful quitting.

Humans greatly dislike a psychological state called cognitive dissonance. Cognitive means to do with the mind or thoughts. Dissonance means conflict. So cognitive dissonance refers to a state of mind in which a person has conflicting thoughts about something. A clear example of this would be the two thoughts 'Smoking causes cancer' and 'I smoke'. Or 'vaping messes up mental health' and 'I vape'. Or 'I don't want to smoke forever' and 'I can't quit'.

Cognitive dissonance often arises when people are secretly unhappy about the way they have behaved or are behaving. The same process can be seen in many areas of life. People like to be able to justify their behaviour. We don't much care if we are right, as long as we believe we are right.

Smoking creates massive amounts of cognitive dissonance because people are repeatedly doing something that they know is unhealthy and expensive. People are also aware that they are trapped by addiction. All addicts are in the terrible position of continuing with a behaviour that scares them, destroys their health, costs them lots of money, and interferes with day-to-day life.

To add to their miseries, they seem to get so little in return for these devastating financial, physical and emotional costs. I mean why *do* people smoke or vape? There is little physical or emotional change. Smokers do not experience euphoric effects. Nicotine is not an intoxicant. There is no high associated with smoking. The 'buzz' or 'head rush' very young or inexperienced smokers describe simply reflects an intolerance to nicotine, which vanishes when they become addicted. And in the case of cigarettes, they don't even taste nice.

When you first start to smoke tobacco you experience smoking as revolting and horrible. And the cigarettes don't change. They taste as horrible after ten years as they did at first. If you have 'developed a taste' for them, this is just another example of changing beliefs instead of behaviour. Don't believe me? Have you tasted one recently?

Let's do a behavioural experiment. Light one now - go on, I'll wait. In fact you'd better smoke two. The first one will get rid of Nitch, who disguises the taste.

Ready with the second cigarette? Ten deep drags - hold each one - focus intently on the taste and sensation. Mmmmm?

Vapes overcome the revolting taste issue to a degree. At least until vile vape liquid spits at you, or you experience the horrible taste of a burnt coil. But inhaling sweet-flavoured vapour is not the reason anyone does it. If it was, why bother with the risks of nicotine. People can enjoy aromatherapy, but no-one is hooked on it.

Since smoking and vaping attract enormous costs, and offer remarkably little in return, smokers find themselves in the very uncomfortable position of behaving in a way they don't like. They need to relieve this discomfort, and they do this by developing strong and powerful beliefs about the benefits and pleasures of smoking and vaping.

This is where Nitch's propaganda machine comes in. You need a justification to puff. And Nitch is only too happy to provide you with hundreds of them.

Remember the benefits and pleasures of smoking we talked about earlier? Well, that is Nitch at his best. He manages to make you believe that cigarettes/e-cigs calm you down, sharpen you up, help you focus, help you unwind, aid your concentration, keep you alert, help you sleep, enhance your enjoyment of any activity, ease the pain of any misfortune, and provide pleasure and satisfaction.

Smokers come to believe that, okay, they aren't happy about the health stuff, but, hey, smoking does so much for them! If they didn't smoke, they couldn't work, enjoy themselves or relax. They would be grumpy and miserable all the time, for ever and ever. Faced with a choice of quitting and being irritable and miserable, or keeping on smoking, people usually choose smoking. But the secret of successful stopping is that you don't have to feel miserable and deprived if you stop.

It cannot be emphasised enough that the benefits are costs in disguise. And it is so easy to be fooled because they are widely regarded, not just by smokers, but by non-smokers, and even by some health professionals, as genuine effects of smoking.

The questionnaire that you filled in was adapted from a widely accepted and much-used questionnaire developed by a respected scientist called Tomkins in 1966. He called it the Reasons for Smoking Scale. Turn back and look at it again. The scientist who came up with all those reasons for smoking believed that they were genuine effects of smoking. If a top scientist in the field was fooled by all this, no wonder you believe it too. And if you are thinking, 'well that was 1966, the world has moved on,' the very similar Modified Reasons for Smoking Scale was developed in 2003, to help clinicians assess the smoker's motivations to smoke. [1] Items included increasing positive feelings (cigarettes don't), reducing negative feelings, (cigarettes don't), and aspects like handling and taste (which are irrelevant). That measure remains in regular use.

The secret of successful quitting is to understand that these are not reasons for smoking, but justifications for smoking to make you feel better about it.

Key Concept

'Reasons' for smoking are really justifications to make you feel better about it.

The tragedy about developing these inaccurate beliefs is that they then present a formidable barrier to quitting. A person isn't just giving up an anti-social, unhealthy and expensive behaviour, but a highly valued, stress-relieving, confidence-enhancing, ever-reliable friend.

The joy of quitting is the recognition that all these perceived benefits are false promises, and that when you stop you find yourself finally able to truly enjoy the benefits that you thought cigarettes gave you. Quitting delivers what cigarettes promised.

In the doctoral research study I carried out in 1998 I gave people the Reasons for Smoking Questionnaire before and after treatment that aimed to change their positive view of smoking. The good news is that the research showed that these beliefs can easily be altered.

Summary of Nitch's Sneaky Methods:

The feelings of anxiety that Nitch creates when he wants feeding are nicotine withdrawal symptoms. Withdrawal is not something you go through when you are quitting. Withdrawal is what you are going through all day every day, and will continue to go through all day every day for as long as you continue to smoke. You cannot get 'relief' unless you first experience the mild stress of lowered nicotine. You can't have the aaaaahhhhhh without first experiencing ARGGHHH!

Smoking is a hopelessly doomed attempt to get rid of Nitch. He stresses you out and makes you anxious. So you smoke to make him go away. But by smoking you keep him alive, ready and willing to come back to stress you out and make you anxious again.

The feeling of stress can be subtle, but despite this, the drive to relieve it is very powerful. That drive is fuelled by a basic misunderstanding: Your unconscious mind thinks that anxiety = danger and you are motivated to do **whatever it takes** to reduce anxiety. So you smoke. But the danger signals are faulty. The misunderstanding has conned you into smoking, which makes you feel uncomfortable because you know how harmful smoking is to your health.

Nitch doesn't want you to be too worried about these things in case they persuade you to stop his supply of nicotine. He therefore convinces you that the fears are exaggerated or somehow don't apply to you, while at the same time putting cigarettes and e-cigs on a pedestal. This means that when you think about quitting, you fear that you will lose something precious and irreplaceable, rather than recognising you are simply getting rid of an unwelcome intruder, who stresses you out and makes you miserable.

Key Concept

All you are doing when you smoke is trying to get rid of Nitch. But by smoking you are keeping him alive.

Quitting can be easy!

As we saw in Chapter 1, almost everyone knows the hard ways of giving up smoking. Many people have tried them already, and most of them have failed. The easy ways are less well known, although hundreds of thousands of people stumble on them accidentally.

Stopping smoking is simply a matter of killing Nitch off once and for all. By smoking, you get rid of him for a little while. By quitting you get rid of him forever.

But before you kill him you need to understand how he gets your mind to play tricks on itself. You need to rid yourself of his propaganda. If you win the propaganda war, the rest is easy. Most quit attempts fail because the attempt is made despite continuing to believe in his propaganda. In white knuckle quitting the focus is on reasons for stopping. But people still believe in the benefits and pleasures of smoking or vaping. As a result, when they quit, they believe that they are depriving themselves of something they really want and need.

Unless you see through Nitch's propaganda, you will feel miserable, deprived and scared. Which is exactly how Nitch wants you to feel, because he needs you to start smoking again.

Nitch has wormed his way deep into your mind and can maintain a running commentary whose sole purpose is to keep you feeding him:

- I can't live without it.

- I would never be able to work properly.

- Quitting is too hard.

- I will be deprived of all the things I currently enjoy.

- A little of what you fancy does you good.

- I'll quit tomorrow.

- I could get run over by a bus tomorrow.

- It's my only pleasure.

- It takes my mind off all my problems.

- I'll wait till I'm less stressed before I quit.

- I'll never be able to relax again.

- Once a smoker, always a smoker.

- It won't happen to me.

- The money isn't important.

- Who wants to be some sort of health nut anyway?

- I deserve a treat.

and so on and so on ...

This book will help you to develop a new understanding of smoking. It will help explode the myths about cigarettes and expose smoking for what it really is. Nicotine causes anxiety. The need to keep nicotine levels topped up impair concentration and creates huge distractions. Nicotine destroys confidence and self-esteem. And the need to feed Nitch, however inconvenient, is a monumental pain in the backside.

Smoking gets rid of Nitch for a while. Quitting gets rid of Nitch forever.

Chapter Summary

- Being a nicotine addict can be seen as playing host to Nitch.

- Nitch has two weapons:

  - The ability to make you anxious through withdrawal symptoms.

  - Propaganda to distort your beliefs and attitudes to smoking and vaping, to make sure you keep feeding him.

- Nitch gets away with this because:

  - We don't recognise that he makes us anxious.

  - We are actively looking for excuses to justify our smoking.

Chapter 5:
How Does It All
Start? Addiction

Is nicotine truly addictive? And does that mean you are a drug addict? Yes and yes! Even the tobacco companies have known that nicotine is addictive since at least the 1960s, despite their continued attempts to deny this publicly. This is revealed in a series of internal documents anonymously leaked and published in 1995 [1]. In an internal paper in 1963, the vice-president of Brown & Williamson Tobacco Corporation (BW), which is owned by the British American Tobacco Company (BAT), writes: 'Nicotine is addictive, we are therefore in the business of selling nicotine, an addictive drug.'

BAT and BW have also known since at least the 1970s that smoking 'light' cigarettes is completely ineffective at reducing the risks of smoking because smokers will automatically take more or deeper drags in order to regulate administration of nicotine: 'Whatever the characteristics of cigarettes ... the smoker adjusts his pattern to deliver his own nicotine requirements.' Filtered cigarettes were also known to be ineffective for the same reason. 'The smoker of a filter cigarette was getting as much or more nicotine and tar as he would have done from a regular cigarette.'

This is true for lower nicotine percentage vape liquids too. Most disposable bars like crystal or elf bars have 20mg of nicotine (or 2%), which is also the standard amount for most vape liquids. But you can buy 1% or 0.5% liquids which people believe might help them quit. But they just smoke far more to compensate.

The US Surgeon General was slower to recognise this than the tobacco industry, and even today many smokers believe that switching to a 'light' or low nicotine brand is an effective way of reducing their risk - a misconception that the tobacco industry has exploited effectively through advertising. For example, the advert for True Cigarettes in 1975 ran: 'All the fuss about smoking got me thinking I'd either quit, or I'd smoke True. I smoke True.'

But what does the word 'addiction' actually mean?

Behaviours get the label of addiction when the costs of continuing the behaviour - for example, disease, death, financial ruin, self disgust and shame - clearly outweigh the pleasures and benefits. Some people feel uncomfortable about putting smokers in this category because smoking is so widespread and acceptable.

But history has shown that nicotine has been consumed compulsively in nearly every culture into which it has been introduced. On the other hand, every nicotine-free cigarette that has ever been marketed has been a complete commercial failure.

Historical accounts also show the extreme lengths people will go to so that they can smoke. During the occupation in Holland in the Second World War there was widespread starvation in many cities, but nonetheless many people chose to grow tobacco instead of food, and in concentration camps cigarettes were often exchanged for food. In post-war Europe people stole and prostituted themselves to obtain tobacco. And in case you were in any further doubt about the power of nicotine addiction, Murad the Cruel of Turkey (1609-40) had smokers beheaded, hanged and quartered. In Romania smokers were flogged and exiled to Siberia, while in Japan in 1616 smokers were imprisoned and had their property confiscated. None of these measures stopped people smoking.

Consider the following facts:

- 92% of GPs believe that nicotine is powerfully addictive, half believing it to be more addictive than heroin or cocaine.

- 30% of smokers try to quit every year, but only 2-3% succeed.

- 60% of smokers smoke after a heart attack, 40% of them within forty-eight hours.

- 50% of smokers smoke again after surgery to remove their larynx.

- 50% of smokers smoke again after surgery to remove sections of lung.

- 80% of pregnant smokers continue to smoke throughout pregnancy.

Key Concept

Nicotine is one of the most addictive substances on Earth.

Believe it or not, cigarettes are so addictive that research has shown that over 90% of teenagers who smoke four cigarettes become regular smokers, and that the vast majority of these smokers will smoke for the rest of their lives.[2] That's all it takes. A lifetime of misery, cost and ill health for the sake of four measly cigarettes. And the worst irony of all is that those kids don't even enjoy those first four life-wrecking cigarettes.

The word 'addiction' is used if a drug has certain characteristics or leads to certain behaviours: Withdrawal, tolerance, dependence and intoxication. The first 3 are generally seen as proxy indicators for addictiveness, while intoxication is not, but is associated with greater harms caused by the drug.

There are significant differences between drugs on all those domains. [3]

Drugs can behave very differently from each other. Some drugs are highly addictive and some are not. Some involve obvious mind and mood-altering effects and some do not. Drugs act on different brain pathways. As everyone's brain is wired differently, and we are talking about complex interactions between drugs and brains, I can only talk in generalities. Not everyone will experience these drugs in the same way. But overall, there are clear differences in the way drugs affect us. And to simplify matters you can think of drugs acting on PLEASURE pathways in the brain and/or acting on ADDICTION pathways in the brain.

These 2 processes are **NOT THE SAME!!**

Some drugs are experienced as pleasurable and some are not. An indicator of this 'pleasure' could be the level of intoxication experienced. The high, the buzz, the release.

Drugs also vary in terms of addiction, and you can use measures of dependence or tolerance for this.

Nicotine scores extremely high for dependence and yet very low for intoxication. This is because nicotine has a high dependency value with a low intoxication value: High addiction, low pleasure. Nicotine is not pleasurable, each cigarette or vape merely relieves the stress of the previous one. Nicotine really does nothing for anyone, but it is highly addictive, which drives people to seek it out and use it compulsively.

Then you have a drug like cannabis: High intoxication value, low dependency value: i.e. high pleasure, low addiction. People can enjoy the sensations of being stoned, can smoke quite heavily for a while, but walk away from it without a backwards glance. In fact, many people inadvertently get hooked on the nicotine in joints, even though they assume they are just smoking for the effects of the cannabis. Many a stoner has found themselves rolling ever weaker joints, until finally they are just rolling cigs. They can leave the cannabis behind but find themselves still needing to smoke for the nicotine.

And then there are the drugs which scores high on both, like alcohol or heroin. Alcohol and heroin act on both pleasure pathways and the addiction pathways.

This process is beautifully illustrated in Richard Feynman's book: *Surely You're Joking Mr Feynman*. Feynman was a professor of Physics and widely recognised as a genius. Earlier in his book he makes reference to drinking: meeting girls, hanging out in bars, enjoying the way the bartender always had 'his' drink ready for him – a perk of being a regular.

He was lecturing in Brazil for 10 months, staying in a hotel used by stewardesses from Pan Am with whom he spent a lot of time. He wrote:

"The people from the Airlines were somewhat bored with their lives, strangely enough, and at night they would often go to the bars to drink. I liked them all, and in order to be sociable, I would go with them to the bar to have a few drinks several nights a week. One day, about 3:30 in the afternoon, I was walking along the sidewalk opposite the beach at Copacabana past a bar. I suddenly got this tremendous, strong feeling: "That's just what I want; that'll fit just right. I'd just love to have a drink right now!"

I started to walk into the bar, and I suddenly thought to myself, "Wait a minute! It's the middle of the afternoon. There's nobody here. There's no social reason to drink. Why do you have such a terribly strong feeling that you have to have a drink?" – and I got scared. I never drank ever again since then. I suppose I really wasn't in any danger because I found it very easy to stop. But that strong feeling that I didn't understand frightened me."

Feynman was a genius, an incredible thinker. He recognised the urges that arose from the addiction pathways in his brain were alien to himself. HE wanted to have social drinks with pretty Pan AM stewardesses! Booze Itch just wanted the alcohol.

How many of us would have noticed this? How many would have just walked into the bar, suppressing any disquiet, and allowing ourselves to be taken in by the Booze Itch narrative of 'I want a drink because I enjoy a drink. It's a sunny day. I've been working hard. I'm at the beach. Just the place and time for a nice cold beer'. And thereby started down that rabbit hole of confusing WANTING a drink with the PLEASURE of drinking.

What also confuses the picture is that we are complex social beings. We can become psychologically dependent on things we are not chemically dependent on. And conversely, we can develop positive beliefs about drugs we don't enjoy but ARE dependent on, which then convince us we truly enjoy them.

Yet another complication is that most other people are also confused about the difference between *wanting* nicotine and *liking* nicotine. Even researchers and clinicians who treat smokers.

Being truly free from drug dependency means ending the chemical dependency AND changing your thinking and perceptions around the drug.

The Spectrum of Dependence

When we start using nicotine, the drug is acting on dependency pathways, leading to a desire for the drug that is entirely brain based, and nothing to do with any quality of the nicotine: you want the drug because pathways in your brain send signals asking for it.

Most of us are not like Professor Feynman. Feynman enjoyed drinking while socialising but, unknown to him, he was also developing a dependency, and this is what triggered a strong craving to drink that afternoon. He recognised that feeling as different to the reason he himself was enjoying a drink, and ended his relationship with booze there and then.

However, us ordinary mortals are not so insightful or self-aware. We experience the desire and just think 'I want to smoke because I like it'. As we increasingly desire, need, and seek out nicotine, we find ways to rationalise that need. And soon we can find ourselves saying 'I'm dying for a puff', 'I really need a cig', without any concern at all about WHY we experience such strong urges for a drug that does not even appear to really do anything.

There are individual differences in how quickly pathways are activated, but once dependency has begun to develop, nicotine acts on the addiction centres of your brain causing them to prompt you to seek out nicotine again. You are aware that you 'want to' vape or 'feel like' a cigarette. You are NOT aware that this 'I want a smoke' feeling – a vague sense of dissatisfaction or emptiness that disappears when you smoke or vape – is driven by dependency and not pleasure.

We don't notice we are becoming dependent for 2 main reasons:

1) It is a very subtle process at first. The 'I want to smoke' feeling is so similar to other normal wants and wishes that we do not recognise the anxious/empty feeling that lies behind it. Not at first anyway.

2) Once we DO begin to recognise that 'gasping for a smoke' may be an unhealthy sign of a growing dependency we reject any idea that we are becoming dependent out of hand. And we can carry on rejecting evidence of dependency for years. Even decades. No-one wants to believe that they are dependent, so we automatically develop a whole host of mental strategies to convince ourselves that we are fine, our behaviour is under control, and we are perfectly safe to carry on as we are.

It can be hard to understand, but pleasure and addiction have nothing to do with one another. Smoking is addictive. Cigarettes are addictive. Vapes are addictive. Even though the feeling of stress from withdrawal can be very subtle. That means the first cigarette you ever smoke is addictive, as is the first vape you puff. The confusion arises because people do not really understand how addiction works.

A defining feature of addiction is so-called compulsive use. In other words, you feel that you cannot do without whatever it is you are addicted to. You might think that if you do not enjoy something, then you could easily do without it. If you could easily do without it, then you cannot be addicted. You are therefore safe to continue 'experimenting' or impressing your friends, or whatever else it is you think you are doing. While you are not really enjoying it, it cannot be dangerous. Right? **WRONG!**

This seems to make sense, but unfortunately this logic is wrong. If it were true, then no one would ever get hooked. Cigarettes do not politely tap you on the shoulder and say, 'excuse me, you have hated the taste of me so far, but the next cigarette will be like nectar from heaven, and once you have tasted it you will never be able to give me up.' The first cigarette tastes bad, the fifth cigarette tastes bad and the fifty-thousandth cigarette tastes bad. Addiction has nothing to do with taste or pleasure.

You don't get hooked on vapes just because they taste nice. If we were hooked on the taste of the vape we would be addicted to things like flavoured water. All the flavours do is remove one of the barriers to starting in the first place, which is why they are so popular with kids, who instinctively loathe tobacco based cigarettes.

What is really going on?

When you first smoke as a youngster, you have no nicotine in your body. You therefore have no Nitch. The first cigarette puts nicotine into your body. As the nicotine leaves, you are left feeling a tiny bit stressed. Nicotine withdrawal is unpleasant from the day you start smoking, but the effects are tiny at first. Think of nicotine like paint stripper. Except instead of dissolving paint, nicotine dissolves good feelings. And as it leaves your body it takes those good feelings with it. When you smoke your second cigarette two things happen:

1) The toxins in the cigarette make you cough or feel sick, and you experience the cigarette as horrible, just like the first one.

2) At the same time, the good feelings that the last cigarette dissolved away are restored.

Then you put out your second cigarette, and nicotine leaves your body, taking with it good feelings and leaving you feeling very slightly anxious.

What makes nicotine addiction so confusing is that nicotine withdrawal is so subtle. No two smokers describe exactly the same thing, and the symptoms that are described tend to be vague psychological-ish ones like irritability and tension. This has led some smoking cessation advisers to conclude that nicotine withdrawal is almost entirely psychological.

This is wrong. Nicotine withdrawal is no less real just because it manifests itself in vague psychological or mental ways, rather than with clear physiological or bodily reactions like the 'cold turkey' seen in heroin withdrawal.

Alternatively, advisers suggest that nicotine withdrawal is trivial because it is no more than mild anxiety. This is a misunderstanding. Even if anxiety is mild, people find it distressing and they are extremely motivated to reduce it. Anxiety may not be painful or harmful, but people still have a very strong desire to get rid of it.

As we saw in Chapter 4, anxiety is essential for our survival, as we equate anxiety with danger, and a reduction in anxiety with safety/survival. When our ancestors were out chasing woolly bears to eat, anxiety was useful. When we are walking along a steep ridge with a big drop on either side, anxiety is useful. When we are confronted by a hissing cobra, anxiety is useful. But what happens when our brain gets confused, and anxiety symptoms are triggered in situations where they are not useful? Remember, anxiety is a biological response. Your survival brain is not rationally weighing up the reasonableness of anxiety - it is just reacting.

With nicotine withdrawal the danger signal is chemically induced and entirely artificial. It is not remotely useful to you. In effect your danger signal is malfunctioning, and danger warnings are flashing every time you run low on nicotine. You can tell yourself logically that there is nothing to worry about - but the biological anxiety system is not logical. Your biological systems cannot tell the difference between useful anxiety that alerts us to danger, and useless anxiety that serves no purpose. It all feels the same: we experience a powerful drive to reduce it by whatever means possible, and you have learned that smoking gets rid of it. But in fact, all you have done by smoking is to reset a faulty signal, so it will go off again next time you are in the same situation.

What can you do differently?

- You need to unlearn that smoking is the right thing to do in response to these danger signals, which are communicated to you via anxiety.

- You need to allow the danger signal to burn itself out and gradually fade away.

If you were hungry and you ignored hunger signals you would get more and more hungry until you were starving. Eventually you would die. But if you ignore faulty anxiety signals, at first the anxiety will also intensify, but gradually it will dawn on your subconscious mind that nothing bad is happening to you, anxiety will fade away, and will gradually disappear.

You cannot talk yourself out of anxiety. It is not responsive to reassurance. All you can do is use logical reasoning to make sure you understand that the only way to free yourself from nicotine addiction is to override the danger signal. But you will feel anxious. You will have to go through a process of nicotine withdrawal to get over smoking. The only way out is through.

You need to allow yourself to go through the anxiety instead of getting rid of it temporarily with nicotine. This then re-wires your brain, so it stops sending you faulty danger signals.

This process is temporary. At the end of it you will be completely free of nicotine. Any residual 'cravings' will then just be psychological.

Key Concept

Nicotine withdrawal is a short-term process. If you ignore the desire to smoke, nicotine will leave your body within a few days.

The anxiety symptoms themselves are not painful, or even particularly unpleasant. In extreme sports people use the thrill of the anxiety symptoms to have fun, to override danger signals for kicks. In bungee jumping you know perfectly well that you are securely tied to the cord and that you cannot fall, but this knowledge makes no difference to your biological anxiety response. Anxiety symptoms may be mild and vague, but we are powerfully motivated to get rid of them.

This is why you will still experience a compulsion to smoke, despite all logical explanations of what is happening. This is also why Nicotine Replacement Therapy (NRT), such as patches, can help, as it takes the edge off this anxiety, while you go through the task of removing the psychological dependence and the habitual aspects of smoking. Chapter 10 provides much more information about NRT.

People are wrong about not getting hooked in the first place. They are also wrong, time and time again, about not getting re-addicted after quitting for a while. Many people who have experienced the misery of being hooked think, 'It won't happen again, this time I will stay in control.'

You were never in control in the first place! If you are to have any chance of lifelong quitting you need to get rid of the idea that nicotine is somehow controllable and that this time you can handle it. You can't.

Key Concept

Nicotine withdrawal causes anxiety. To withdraw successfully from nicotine, you need to override the danger signal, and ignore the powerful drive to reduce anxiety.

If you keep taking in nicotine, you will reset the danger signal, and anxiety will keep coming back.

Taking up smoking

The most common reason for people to take up smoking is by experimenting in childhood or adolescence. Young people may be tempted to try smoking to impress their friends, out of curiosity, to rebel against parents, or because they see other people smoking and believe it is enjoyable. Peer pressure is also very important. There are, however, some people who do not take up smoking until later in life.

In the case of vapes, peer pressure and curiosity remain the main reason, but much younger children vape than smoke, because vape flavours are designed to be appealing to kids.

Adult experimentation

Some people start smoking or vaping at college, university, or later in life because close friends or partners smoke. This usually either stems from a desire to be sociable or happens because even non-smokers believe that smoking has benefits. If you are feeling stressed, it is natural to turn to something you think might help you.

Vaping seems to have made adult experimentation much more common, perhaps because people don't instinctively loathe vapes like they do cigarettes, and young adults are increasingly getting themselves hooked on various nicotine products, like Snus.

Drug use

Becoming addicted to nicotine is a physical process. If you smoke cannabis and mix the cannabis with tobacco, then you will get hooked on the nicotine in the tobacco. This happens even if you have never had any interest in smoking cigarettes, and even if you are only smoking because you like the effects of cannabis.

It may take a while to realise you are hooked, and most drug users believe that it is the cannabis they are getting hooked on, when they start craving joints. The penny usually drops when someone is running low on cannabis and starts rolling ever weaker joints, until they are just rolling tobacco. They then discover that the cannabis-free 'joint' does them very nicely thank-you. The message from this is that when you stop smoking, you need to stop every form of nicotine use.

The solution

You need to reset the faulty danger signal by killing Nitch. But first you need to understand his other weapon: propaganda, which causes psychological dependence. This is discussed in the next chapter.

Chapter Summary

- Nitch's first weapon is anxiety. He uses anxiety to push us around.

- The anxiety is vague but our unconscious mind sees it as a danger signal.

- We are therefore powerfully motivated to get rid of it - so we feel driven to smoke or vape.

- Stopping all forms of nicotine will allow this faulty signal to fade away.

- This should then be the end of the problem; but the misunderstanding about why we are driven to smoke gives Nitch a second weapon - propaganda.

Chapter 6:
The Second Weapon-
Propaganda

Nitch can physically stress you out. But he can do a lot more than that. Nitch can get into your head and tell you stuff that simply is not true. How does he get away with it?

We have already talked about Nitch creating anxiety whenever his nicotine levels run a little low. This anxiety triggers a powerful drive to smoke or vape, because your survival brain believes that the anxiety means that you are in danger and directs you to reduce the anxiety (and therefore the danger) by having a cigarette or e-cig. But smokers have absolutely no idea that they are smoking in response to a biological drive. I call this the **fundamental misconception**. It has two stages:

1) Smokers notice that they experience relief when they puff, but do not realise that it was Nitch who was making them anxious in the first place.

2) The feeling of relief is so subtle that it does not seem important enough to explain a behaviour that is as devastating and expensive as smoking.

The apparent benefits of smoking seem so clear because anxiety levels are reduced immediately by smoking, whereas anxiety levels only increase slowly when you are not smoking.

This means that a) you don't notice this pattern, and b) even if you did, it is impossible to tell that it is to do with the last cigarette you smoked. People therefore have no idea why they really smoke. But they are well aware that they do, even though they don't understand why. So they are in a state of conflict. After all, what are the experiences of a nicotine addict?

- The relief of mild anxiety (too mild to be a particularly big deal)

- The knowledge of the dangerousness of smoking or vaping

- The expense of smoking

AND

- The powerful drive to smoke

Smokers therefore make sense of this powerful drive by developing reasons to explain the behaviour, which then develop into positive beliefs.

Key Concept

Smokers don't understand the drive to smoke, so they develop positive beliefs about smoking that provide an explanation. This is the fundamental misconception.

Unfortunately, these beliefs then make people feel deprived if they quit. To quit successfully, you need to change your internal script and develop a new way of thinking about cigarettes and smoking.

Propaganda

When people find themselves behaving in ways they don't like, they feel extremely uncomfortable. This is known as cognitive dissonance, a state where people have conflicting thoughts about something.

To reduce the discomfort, people are highly motivated to find justifications for the behaviour. They want to find excuses that make the behaviour seem okay. These excuses are not necessarily a reflection of reality. In this game, the truth doesn't matter - it's how the beliefs make you feel that counts.

Key Concept

People need to be able to justify their own behaviour. If they don't know the real reasons, they will invent some. This is not a conscious process.

My area of specialism within clinical psychology is Cognitive Behaviour Therapy (CBT), which has been extremely successful in highlighting and exploring the links between thoughts and feelings. People tend to think that their own thoughts are accurate reflections of the world around them. In our own minds our thoughts are intuitively and self-evidently true. But, in fact, our thinking can be highly distorted, and miles away from external reality.

We do not passively receive and process information and then make up our minds about what to think and feel. We actively construct our own worlds. For example, we see what we want and expect to see. We pay close attention to things that fit with our existing views and tend to disregard information that contradicts those views. A good example of this is how sports fans view refereeing decisions. Decisions that go against their team are seen as outrageous and biased, while decisions that go against the opposition are seen as just and fair. (Though strangely this never happens to my team, who are always hard done by!)

Key Concept

We all actively construct our world. We quite literally see what we want and expect to see.

What does this have to do with smoking? A simple example of

how this affects smoking is to compare how afraid you are of smoking in different contexts. If you are at a party, surrounded by other smokers, it is easy to dismiss fears of the health risks of smoking. If you are outside a hospital having a swift smoke before your appointment with a cancer doctor, fears are much harder to dismiss. The reality of the damage you are doing to yourself doesn't change. What changes is how you feel about that reality, and even what you believe about that reality.

Some people will readily accept that smoking is doing them serious physical harm when they are sitting in a GP's surgery being given clear information about the dangers of smoking. But later on, even on the same day, they will be throwing doubt on that information when they are with other smoking friends:

- What do doctors know? They are always getting things wrong.

- Most doctors smoke like chimneys, so who are they to tell me what to do?

- Doctors are just doom merchants, they say everything is bad for you. And they keep changing their minds anyway.

There is research evidence that clearly shows the effects of cognitive dissonance on beliefs and attitudes to smoking. For example, people who have not yet tried to quit are more concerned about the health consequences than people who have made a past quit attempt and failed. Why? Because people who have failed to quit experience more cognitive dissonance than people who still believe they can quit.

Smokers who have never tried to quit have the thoughts 'Smoking causes cancer' and 'I smoke'. This creates dissonance. How can this dissonance be reduced? Well, one way is to develop a third thought, which is: 'I will definitely quit some time'.

But people who have tried and failed to quit don't have the luxury of this third thought. Instead, they have the thoughts 'Smoking causes cancer', 'I smoke' and 'I can't stop smoking'.

This creates greater dissonance, which must be reduced, and the only way is to change their attitudes about the first thought - the health costs. If you have greater amounts of cognitive dissonance you have to go to greater lengths to reduce it by denying that the costs of smoking are real or relevant. This is not rational. But it is what most smokers do. This process is not conscious. It happens totally automatically.

Thinking errors

What I call thinking errors refers to thoughts that are in some way inaccurate, distorted or biased. They offer a solution to cognitive dissonance. Having different thoughts about how dangerous smoking is in different situations is one example of distorting or denying reality.

There are many types of thinking errors.

Minimisation

This is typified by a 'don't worry, be happy' frame of mind. Minimising means playing down the consequences of smoking, for example telling yourself that you've got to die some time, or that serious illnesses don't worry you, or that money is irrelevant, or that you wouldn't want to live forever anyway.

It is important to remember that the distorted thoughts you have about smoking won't seem distorted to you - they will seem entirely plausible and self-evidently true. You must be ruthlessly honest with yourself. Don't accept your own thinking and rationalising at face value.

Smokers die an average of 10 years early. And several years before that are blighted by COPD, cancer or heart and lung disease. Think of someone you know who has died of a smoking-related disease. What would those 10 extra years have meant to them, to you, to their families? Think of an elderly non-smoker who died. Imagine losing the last ten years with them, and another 5 years before that lost to disease. How much precious life would they have missed?

After you reach 40, each additional year you smoke reduces your life expectancy by another three months: you are literally shortening your life by a quarter, each and every year.

Vaping is unhealthy too. It is already known that vaping is associated with severe lung disease, including Spontaneous Lung Collapse, Lipoid Pneumonia and possibly Popcorn Lung in countries where vapes are permitted to contain Diacetyl. These can affect very young vapers. Vapes are filled with chemicals, many known to be carcinogenic (cancer forming). Vaping is a fairly new behaviour, and long term studies do not yet exist, but evidence of harm is emerging all the time.

Many people minimise smoking. This is not because smokers are happy-go-lucky, laid-back people. Even smokers who think they are realistic about the dangers are more than likely kidding themselves. They might believe it intellectually, but this knowledge has little emotional impact. When I smoked I believed virtually everyone who smoked died of it in the end. Then I read that in fact one in four smokers died from smoking (as was thought at that time. It is now thought to be 1 in 2). I was genuinely happy about this! I thought that those odds were pretty good so I could stop worrying about it.

If you are thinking, 'Well, those are good odds,' contrast that with concern about other health scares. People become terribly worried about contracting other diseases, but the odds against dying of them are many thousands to one. With smoking the odds are 50:50! Smokers have to insulate themselves from the dangers of smoking, because otherwise the cognitive dissonance would be too high to bear.

Minimising the financial costs is also very common. But this does not mean smokers are more generous than average, and happy to throw their money around. When smokers say money isn't important, they are usually referring exclusively to money for cigarettes or vapes. They are not saying they would be happy to pay over the odds for their shopping, or for petrol, or for insurance, or for holidays abroad, or indeed for anything at all except smoking.

So money is important in every other area of life. It is not them who don't mind spending the money - it's Nitch. He doesn't think the money is important, but then he's not the one spending it!

Denial

Denial, or the 'ostrich syndrome', is like minimisation, but takes it a step further. Rather than thinking, 'Well it might happen, but so what', people in denial simply assume that it will not happen to them. Smokers receive large amounts of smoking-related information from a variety of sources. These include doctors, magazines, newspapers, advertisements, personal experience, conversations with other people, television images, books and so on. If we were entirely rational beings we would treat all incoming material equally. We would register the information, assess the reliability of the source and make a balanced judgement about how credible or true this information is.

However, we do no such thing. We usually notice or seek out information that fits with what we already believe. If we are given information that we don't like, we just ignore it. Thoughts include:

- They say everything gives you cancer these days.

- If I didn't smoke or vape, I'd be more stressed so my health would suffer.

- My uncle lived to eighty and he smoked two packs a day.

- Statistics don't mean anything.

- I eat well and exercise so I'm pretty healthy really.

- I don't inhale.

- I only smoke menthols.

- Loads of people smoke so it can't be that bad.

- My aunt gave up smoking and developed pneumonia.

In 1964 when the US Surgeon General first published links between smoking and cancer, some research was done on how this information was viewed by the public. Only 10% of non-smokers thought the evidence for links between smoking and cancer was flawed, compared with 40% of smokers. In other words, we often believe what we want to believe rather than making a rational judgement based on the evidence. Cognitive dissonance turns us from rational beings into rationalising beings.

Key Concept

Cognitive dissonance turns us from rational beings into rationalising beings.

You may have seen a programme on television about an expensive health farm. Part of the weekly programme involved a quitting smoking package. A quitter in his thirties was having a medical examination. This involved blowing into a tube to test his lung function. The other smokers were standing around waiting for their turn and the atmosphere was relaxed.

'Well, Mr Smith, let's see how your bellows are doing', says the physiologist cheerfully. After the test he tut-tuts and says, 'Oh dear...' in mock disapproval. Giggles all round. 'Mr Smith, your lungs are about twenty years older than the rest of you!' Mr Smith pulls an 'Oops, silly me' kind of a face and grins ruefully. The rest of the group chuckles.

This was not fiction but real people on a real course. The amazing thing about this scene is how totally inappropriate everybody's emotional responses are. Imagine anyone being given similarly devastating medical information in any other context: a diabetic being told his kidneys were packing up or a miner that he had lung damage.

Any time people are exposed to dangerous substances such as asbestos or silicon they become (quite reasonably) extremely anxious. If subsequent tests show damage the response is fear, anger and disbelief.

But when it comes to damage due to smoking, people treat it like some big joke. This is a classic example of the ostrich syndrome. Smokers ignore and dismiss any scary information, either refusing to believe the dangers, or refusing to think realistically about their implications. This is one reason why shock tactics rarely work to help people quit.

Rose-tinted glasses

Just as we downplay the costs and risks of smoking, so we exaggerate the benefits and put cigarettes and vapes on a pedestal. Even cigarettes that are a downright pain in the neck to smoke - because of the circumstances in which we smoke them - tend to be viewed positively.

Arbitrary inference

Arbitrary inference refers to the fact that we are not very good scientists. A scientist makes careful, unbiased observations and then draws conclusions from them. Most people, however, jump to conclusions on far more flimsy evidence. If we see a smoker who looks fit and healthy we tend to think, 'Well, he seems fine, so smoking can't be that bad.' Or a famous footballer gets papped with an elf bar in hand, leading us to conclude that vaping is perfectly safe. Happy, smiley smokers make us think that smoking is relaxing, pleasant and fun. Yet when we see miserable-looking people smoking we tend to blame their misery on the fact that they are probably homeless, or that it's raining, or that it is Monday morning and they are on their way to work - it never crosses our mind that they might be miserable because they smoke.

Selective attention

This refers to the fact that we do not observe the world in a consistent way. We notice some things far more than others, even if both are equally visible. In other words, our perception is influenced by our current concerns. An example of this is the way that when women become pregnant the world suddenly seems full of other pregnant women. Or that when you learn a new word you start seeing it everywhere. Or when you buy a new car and everyone seems to then have the same car as you.

Selective attention also affects smokers: when you are struggling to cope without cigarettes, the world suddenly seems full of relaxed and happy smokers. In truth, smokers are more miserable, stressed and tense than non-smokers. If your observations tell you different, that's just because you are observing the things you expect to see, and failing to notice other evidence.

Try to reverse this tendency. Next time you are out, carefully watch all smokers and vapers. Not just the handsome, fit, healthy, happy-looking ones, but the coughing, grumpy, wrinkled, miserable-looking ones too.

Inevitability

Some people think that they have no option but to smoke. So they might as well make the best of it. 'I'm an addict and once an addict, always an addict'. But the addictiveness of nicotine does not condemn them to a lifetime of smoking. Everyone who has ever smoked in the past was an addict for as long as they continued to smoke. And millions have successfully quit. Telling yourself that you have no choice is a cop out. Don't let yourself off the hook like that. Yes, you are an addict. But you can stop anyway.

Deal-making/bargaining

When people want something they don't think they should have, they sometimes try to bargain with themselves. Some people even use bargaining or deal-making to persuade themselves to stop smoking in the first place. Once, when I was still a smoker, I realised that I was sick of feeling tired and unhealthy, so I decided to quit smoking and get fit. I started jogging and quickly noticed that I could go a little further every day. This evidence of success was powerfully motivating and for a while my quit attempt went really well.

Unfortunately, I hadn't got rid of any of the positive beliefs about smoking. I thought that I was making a big sacrifice for the sake of my health and, though I was pleased with my progress, I still missed cigarettes. After a while, the nicotine withdrawal was over, and so I should have been free. But I wasn't, because I still thought of cigarettes in a positive way. Gradually I got used to the fact that I could run and it stopped being such a good motivator. I was glad to be fitter, but it wasn't such a big deal any more. The desire for a cigarette began to outweigh the desire to stay stopped. I started thinking, 'I can run four miles now, that'll do. I mean, how fit do I want to be?'

Eventually I made a deal with myself. I was allowed to smoke again, but only after I had exercised that day. In that way I was going to keep fit and still be allowed to smoke. Excellent plan! I even told myself that I would be healthier that way, because any damage done by smoking would be cancelled out by running. I was a medical student at the time and knew that this was utter rubbish. However healthy taking exercise may be, it does not cancel out the effects of smoking. But smokers do not let inconvenient things like reality get in the way of smoking, so I spent the next week or so only smoking after I had been running.

Soon enough the day came when it was raining, and I couldn't be bothered to run. But I wanted to smoke. I was totally back into smoking and couldn't imagine not having a cigarette. So I leapt to my feet, did ten star jumps and then lit up, thinking, 'I've done my exercise so that's okay.'

This episode shows the problem with bargaining. Firstly the trade-off you think you are making is unlikely to reflect reality. And secondly, Nitch is a Bad Faith dealer! If you have done quite well in stopping smoking, just having the odd one seems possible, and any deal that lets you smoke occasionally seems quite good. But as soon as you are smoking regularly, Nitch is back in control, and whatever bargain you originally made won't ever satisfy him. Nitch cannot be bargained with. He'll say absolutely anything to get that first post-quitting cig lit, then go back on the deal. As soon as he gets his foot in the door, he will be blowing it wide open. So do not kid yourself with the false promise of deals and bargains.

Key Concept

Give Nitch an inch, and he will take a mile.

Catastrophisation

This thinking error involves believing the worst about a situation. For a smoker, these might be thoughts like 'If I quit I will never be happy again' or 'Smoking is my best friend, it's all I've got left'.

This sort of statement can feel very powerful but is usually grossly exaggerated. No one is 'never happy again', despite dreadful hardships. Just look around the world and don't exaggerate your difficulties. Quitting is a period of adjustment, following which you will still be you, enjoying the things you enjoy, seeing the people you like to see, doing the things you like to do.

One of the key features of thinking errors is that thoughts feel true to the person having them, no matter how far-fetched. If we say to ourselves, 'I'll never be happy again' or 'everyone hates me' or 'if I fail to get this job, I'm a worthless person and I'll never succeed in life', these thoughts are exaggerated. But we respond emotionally to them as if they were true. We don't have 'exaggeration filters' between our thoughts and our feelings. If we think it, we feel it. Those exaggerated thoughts are just a story you are telling yourself. Drop the story and make sure you don't allow your thoughts to be extreme, exaggerated or catastrophic. Take a bit of a reality check every so often.

As for 'smoking is all I have' - if this is true then you seriously need to quit! Most smokers who describe smoking as their 'best friend' or 'only pleasure' have many friends and family (who may be somewhat offended to think that you consider them irrelevant). Be honest about the things of value in your life. Who do you care about, who cares about you, what do you like doing? Do not give cigarettes status that they do not deserve.

If you really feel very lonely and you do not have any activities that you enjoy, then this is a problem in its own right. You need to try to deal with that problem at the same time as quitting. Smoking is not helping you to make friends and develop social activities. All it is doing is costing you money that you could use far more effectively by joining a club, group or activity, and costing you health, which will make it even harder to get out and about.

Another example of catastrophic thinking is that stopping smoking will prevent you from working. Many people use this as an excuse to continue smoking, believing that if they quit, they will be unable to function. This is also inaccurate. It may be true that when King George V was operated on, his surgeon puffed over the anaesthetised body, but surgeons nowadays are not allowed to smoke in operating theatres. And yet they can carry out many hours of intensely concentrated work, without smoking - even the ones who are heavy smokers.

Surgeons who smoke will come out of theatre after a four-hour operation and immediately light up. They may at that point believe that they need that cigarette. But if the operation took five, six or seven hours they would have had no problem staying focused. You do not need cigarettes to do your job.

Selective memory

This refers to the human tendency to remember things in a biased way. Research has shown that what we can remember depends on factors such as mood, situation and beliefs. If we are happy, we tend to remember other times when we were happy. If we are sad, we remember sad times. When people quit smoking, they remember cigarettes in a biased way.

Most cigarettes and vapes are smoked automatically and are not pleasurable. Some cigarettes are actively horrible. But when we quit we forget about those ones. Instead, we remember the 'good' cigarettes, such as smokes we had after a long period of not smoking, or those when we are out having fun. As a result many people quit, then say I'm just going to have a vape on a night out, or a quick puff of a friend's vape. Eventually friends get annoyed, but by then you are craving all the time, and end up buying your own nicotine supply.

In a similar way, when we have relapsed after a period of quitting, we forget that quitting wasn't that bad. This is a strange mental trick that allows people to say, 'I can't imagine life without a smoke', even if they had 2 happy nicotine free years in recent memory.

A friend of mine recently quit smoking. For the first three weeks he was fine. He was positive, determined and motivated. For the next four months he continued not to smoke and carried on feeling fine about it. He told me he was really pleased he had stopped and would never go back to smoking again. A week later I saw him lighting up in the pub. He told me he was 'just having the odd one', because he had overcome the addiction and would never go back to regular smoking. I knew he was sunk at that point, but I rarely talk to people about smoking unless they ask for my advice, so I just sadly watched as his 'occasional cigarettes' became more and more frequent. Finally, a few weeks later he bought a packet. He lit up with a sigh of pure rapture, looked lovingly at the glowing end of his cig and said, 'thank goodness I'm smoking again after four months of torture.'

It is important to recognise that he was not deliberately lying. He truly believed his four month abstinence had been terrible, because as a (re)addicted smoker he could not imagine life without smoking. But in reality, he had been absolutely fine.

Co-collusion

This refers to the way smokers talk about smoking or vaping to each other. Nitch's propaganda is triply powerful because there are millions of smokers, all with their own little parasitic Nitches, all being fed propaganda, and all believing it. Your own beliefs are echoed again and again by other people. In addition, smokers will try to support the inaccurate beliefs of other smokers, in the hope that the other smoker will do the same for them. Smokers need to feel better about their smoking. Smoker A makes Smoker B feel better, and Smoker B makes Smoker A feel better in return.

This is illustrated in the following conversation:

'I saw my doctor today. He told me to quit smoking.'

'Don't they always?'

'My chest feels a bit rubbish. But it's only a cold.'

'Doctors drive me mad. They never let smokers get colds or coughs - it is always blamed on smoking.'

'I reckon I get fewer colds than non-smokers I know.'

'Me too. I've always thought germs couldn't survive in my lungs. I smoke 'em out.' (Laughs.)

'Double vodkas do the same thing for my stomach! Drink?'

'Double vodka sounds good'.

'Cig?'

'Cheers, mate.'

> Smokers make many thinking errors about their smoking. These errors make them less likely to quit and more likely to be miserable if they do quit.

Why do people make thinking errors?

Thinking errors have different functions. Selective memory and denial serve the function of protecting you, the smoker, from the dreadful realities of smoking. Or, rather, they protect you from thinking about them - you are still (unfortunately) living the terrible realities.

No one intends or wants to keep smoking or vaping for life. They always believe quitting will be in the fairly near, (but not too near) future. People often despair when the realisation dawns that they are actually hooked. The 'head in the sand' attitude can make a rapid reappearance under these circumstances.

I had a friend at university who smoked. She always said she felt fine about her smoking because she enjoyed it and because it helped her cope with the stresses of her course. However, she did not see herself as a smoking forty-year-old. Smoking was fine, for now, but would not be a habit she continued for much longer. She consistently said that she would stop after her final-year exams. This reassuring belief meant that she could smoke without worrying too much about it, safe in the knowledge that she was going to quit quite soon.

Several months after the exams I met her at a party. Surprise, surprise, she was smoking.

'What happened to quitting?' I asked.

'Oh, I never intended to quit, I like smoking,' she replied.

Now she wasn't lying. She honestly believed that she never intended to quit. Because if she wanted to quit but couldn't, what would that mean? If she couldn't quit, now, today, why would she be able to quit tomorrow or the next day or the day after that?

This reality was so uncomfortable that my friend genuinely erased her plans to quit from memory. When it came to it she felt she could not quit. She did not want to admit that she was hopelessly hooked and so clung to a belief that smoking was a choice: she was smoking because she enjoyed it. Her memory then edited out evidence that smoking was not a choice.

Some thinking errors make you believe you need cigarettes, for example, catastrophisation and putting cigarettes on a pedestal.

All the errors can be viewed as 'propaganda' peddled by Nitch to make you carry on smoking.

Propaganda and quitting

Let's look at the process of quitting again. People tend to focus on their feelings and assume that their thoughts stem from their feelings. For example:

FEELINGS: Misery when I try to stop smoking, results in THOUGHTS: I need to smoke or I will be miserable.

In reality the process works the other way around. Thoughts drive feelings, not vice versa. In other words:

THOUGHTS: I need cigarettes or I will be miserable, leads to FEELINGS: Misery when I don't smoke.

If you change the message in your head, the feelings change too. This is why the same smoker can have different quit experiences if the thoughts are different each time.

> **Key Concept**
>
> Thoughts often drive feelings, not the other way around.

The misery of quitting is not caused by withdrawal symptoms but by the exhausting running commentary in your head: 'Go on, have one, just one won't hurt, you deserve a treat.' To change that destructive internal script, you need to understand how Nitch operates. If you understand the process, you can disarm it. Nitch spouts this nonsense about smoking because his entire existence depends on you lighting up the next cigarette or puffing the next vape. Imagine an alcoholic who thinks, 'drink gives me courage and confidence.' It is obvious to everyone that drink is sapping his courage and confidence, but the alcoholic clings to a belief that is clearly untrue, to justify carrying on drinking. Addicted thinking is faulty thinking, and smokers are just as deluded as any other addicts.

> **Key Concept**
>
> Addicted thinking is faulty thinking.

How can Nitch make us believe all this rubbish if it isn't true? Why is it so easy for him to fool us for so long?

I don't like feeling stupid!

As we have seen, cognitive dissonance is very uncomfortable and the more smoking affects us, the more we need to find reasons to explain why we smoke, and to justify it to ourselves. If you are smoking now, the odds are against you ever stopping, no matter what the cost. The vast majority of smokers smoke for life. This is likely to be just as true of vapers, given that vaping is just inhaling nicotine via vapour instead of smoke. Almost everyone hopes and believes that they will stop one day - just never today! But the cunning nature of Nitch's trap means that as costs rise, the more you believe you need cigarettes or vapes.

Imagine the following situations:

- You are at a party surrounded by relaxed, happy smokers. You light up or puff. Your justification? 'It's sociable and enjoyable. 'Sociability or enjoyment is enough of a reason, because the costs are not immediately obvious in that situation, so you will not be particularly worried about your nicotine habit.

- You are at a party and no one else is smoking or vaping. You go outside, feeling a bit embarrassed. Your justification? 'I want to relax and this helps me. I won't enjoy it so much otherwise.' You need a different reason from 'enjoyment' or 'sociability' because you are not enjoying it much, and you are not being sociable.

- You are at home by yourself. Your justification? 'I'm too stressed without it.'

- You are in hospital and you crawl from your bed dragging your drip-stand down the corridor to stand in the chilly doorway in your night-clothes. Or hide from the nurses in a hospital toilet to zero a vape. Your justification? 'I can't live without it.'

Your reason goes from pleasure (enjoyment) to benefit (relaxation, concentration) to need (can't live/cope without it). No matter what the situation, you feel you want or need *this* cigarette or *this* vape in *this* situation. No matter how bad things get for you, Nitch keeps one step ahead, making you believe you can't live without it. The problem is not the nicotine, it is the power that you give the nicotine. Disarm it now. Change your thinking and Nitch will lose his power.

Chapter Summary

- Nitch's second weapon is propaganda.

- Nicotine addicts do not understand the drive to smoke or vape.

- They do not really enjoy smoking or vaping and they get very little from it.

- But they know they are harmful, expensive and addictive.

- And they know they can't stop thinking about it and fear that they can't quit.

- This causes cognitive dissonance which is uncomfortable.

- People can reduce dissonance by downplaying the risks and elevating the benefits.

- The difficulties of quitting lie in the power you give the cigarettes and vapes, not in qualities of the cigarettes or vapes themselves.

- A secret of successful quitting is to stop giving Nitch so much power.

The next chapter will show you how.

Chapter 7:
Exploding the Myths

We have learned that Nitch has two weapons: stress and propaganda. A basic message of this book is that the pleasures and benefits of taking in nicotine are actually costs in disguise. When I was a smoker, if someone had told me I didn't really enjoy smoking I imagine my reaction would have been along the lines of: 'how on earth can you claim to know how someone else experiences smoking? If I say I enjoy cigarettes and find them relaxing, then smoking is enjoyable and relaxing, and who are you to tell me otherwise?'

This is a perfectly reasonable question, so I'll try to answer it by exploring the supposed pleasures and benefits in detail.

Stress and relaxation

Smoking and vaping help people relax. This 'fact' is almost universally accepted. Even non-smokers who are stressed sometimes say they wished they smoked so that they could have something to help them cope. People are advised to quit during holidays or times when they are less stressed. And quitting approaches often suggest that people learn relaxation techniques so that they can get the benefit of relaxation without needing to smoke. While it is extremely helpful to learn to relax - and 3 of the downloads focus on teaching you deep relaxation techniques, this does not mean that smoking is relaxing and therefore needs replacing.

The 'fact' that cigarettes are relaxing is ingrained so deeply in our culture and psyche that at first it seems absurd to dispute this. 'Everyone knows' smoking calms people down. Some doctors actually recommend that people continue to smoke if they are undergoing severe stress.

But there is not one shred of factual evidence that supports this belief. On the contrary, there is a large body of evidence that shows that smoking is stressful. And that does not just mean that the hardships you have to deal with if you are a smoker, such as the expense and the damage to health, are stressful. It means that smoking itself is stressful.

Nicotine is a stimulant not a relaxant. Smokers are more stressed than non-smokers. Smokers develop stress related illnesses at higher rates than non-smokers. Smokers who quit are less stressed within a short space of time after quitting, and their stress levels carry on dropping long after they quit.

Key Concept

Cigarettes and vapes are stressful, not relaxing.

I am not suggesting for one moment that people don't feel more relaxed after a puff than before it. What I am saying is that people experience this as relaxation, when in fact nicotine causes stress!

Some of you may think I have lost the plot a bit here, but grasping what I have just said is absolutely crucial in understanding (and thereby freeing yourself from) nicotine addiction.

- You experience smoking and vaping as relaxing.

- You feel more relaxed after a cigarette or a puff on a vape.

- But cigarettes and vapes CAUSE stress.

How can all these statements be true?

Consider what happens when you stub out or stop puffing. As we have already seen, nicotine rapidly leaves your body, and you begin to experience the effects of nicotine withdrawal. The effects vary from person to person, but most people feel stressed, tense or restless.

These feelings build up very gradually over time. At first the feelings are so subtle that you barely notice them, but after a while you begin to think about smoking or vaping again. Your body has prompted your brain for more nicotine because the tension has reached a level where it is noticed. These feelings can be summarised by the word anxiety. Anxiety triggers the thought, 'I want a cigarette/vape.' So you have one and instantly feel relieved.

Key Concept

Taking in nicotine appears to be relaxing because this removes the stress that nicotine withdrawal creates.

This happens again and again and again in an unbreaking chain. Nicotine causes anxiety which is relieved by nicotine, which causes anxiety which is relieved by nicotine which causes anxiety which ... on and on and on. This miserable and stressful chain can (and usually does) last a lifetime.

Unless you break it!

The real tragedy about being caught in this nicotine addiction trap is that people forget what being relaxed actually feels like. People are so used to the ever-present stresses and aggravations of life as a smoker that they think they feel normal.

Let's revisit that earlier diagram:

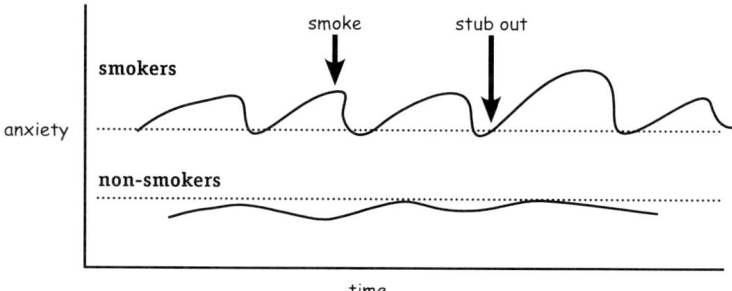

Smokers are withdrawing from nicotine almost **all the time**. Which means that they are enduring the hassle of Nitch's whingeing almost all the time. On the graph notice how the anxiety levels of the smoker rise, then drop sharply when the person smokes. This makes smoking feel satisfying. But notice that the anxiety levels for the smokers are higher all the time than those for non-smokers.

This makes sense because nicotine causes stress and anxiety in many ways:

1) It is a sympathomimetic drug - it stimulates our sympathetic nervous system: or our so-called Fight and Flight system. Anything that activates this system causes us to feel tense and stressed.

2) The health and wealth impacts are anxiety-provoking.

3) The nagging knowledge that you are an addict is stressful.

4) Being a slave to Nitch is very stressful.

Vaping and smoking MAKE YOU ANXIOUS – directly and indirectly.

The feelings of nicotine withdrawal are so much part of smokers' lives that they become the norm. Unless smokers are deprived of cigarettes, when the background low level Nitch whingeing turns into a full-blown Nitch tantrum. They go through the day feeling stressed, and getting rid of the feeling, without ever really being aware of how much tension cigarettes cause. They just think, 'I want a cigarette,' then they have one and think, 'that's better.'

Better than what?

Better than not having one. And why is that?

Because not having one is a source of tension.

Imagine that you want a cigarette or vape but are not able to have one. I'm sure that is a familiar feeling. You feel restless and unsettled and you cannot concentrate on anything. You have a persistent little voice in your head pestering you to work out when/where/how you can get the next hit.

That uncomfortable restless feeling is Nitch. You never had that feeling until you started to smoke. Non-smokers never have that feeling. The feeling was created when you started to smoke, and is being maintained because you continue to smoke. It is an entirely artificial feeling caused by nicotine addiction. That feeling is the feeling of being a smoker. And it is horrible.

Let's do another behavioural experiment. Next time you feel as though you'd like to smoke, just sit with the feeling and pay close attention to how this feeling is experienced in your body and mind. The first step in ending your toxic relationship with nicotine is becoming better at spotting Nitch. Self-monitoring and self-awareness are important to interrupt that habitual re-setting of the faulty alarm. Nitch has you so well trained that you obey him on a whisper, and often don't even know you are feeding HIM, not satisfying yourself. Let's bring some conscious awareness into the process.

Self monitoring exercise

Next time you want a cigarette or e-cig, find somewhere to sit comfortably for a few minutes. In this exercise you are just noticing. Carefully observing your own thoughts, feelings, impulses, urges, sensations and emotions. You are not trying to fix anything or solve anything. You are not trying to create any particular feeling like relaxation. You are just getting in touch with what is going on in your mind and body, and paying attention to it. Where in your body can you feel the 'I want to smoke' urge? What thoughts are popping up? What emotions? In what ways do thoughts, sensations and emotions change over time, as you simply observe the process?

After this exercise, reflect on what you learned, considering the questions:

Can I spot the 'I want a smoke' feeling?

Where can I feel it? Does it move or change?

Can I recognise that feeling as separate from me?

Do urges come and go?

Do thoughts and feelings come and go?

Can I tell the difference between WANTING a smoke and LIKING it?

Self-monitoring helps you spot Nitch so you can stop obeying him. It starts with increased self-awareness.

An example of Nitch-anxiety

I once quit smoking using the willpower method and sweated it out for about ten weeks. It was miserable at first, but over the last two to three weeks I wasn't really thinking about smoking anymore and I felt confident that I had cracked it. So confident that I felt 'safe enough' to smoke a couple when I went out one night. A few days later I smoked a couple more, then more than a couple more. Finally, one Friday when we were out for a drink, my friends insisted I buy my own, so I bought a packet, gave a few away and then went home. I was living alone at the time.

Even though I had been smoking all week, I was still labouring under the delusion that I wasn't a smoker again. I was telling myself that I hadn't really started smoking again, I was just 'being sociable'. But now I was at home on my own with this packet of cigarettes burning a hole in my pocket. If I smoked them, I would be admitting that I was a smoker - even I couldn't pretend that smoking my own cigarettes, by myself in my flat, was a sociable thing to do! I was trying to resist. Trying desperately to resist. But I really, really wanted to smoke.

This voice in my head (aka Nitch) would not shut up:

> 'Have a cig, it's a Friday night, I've had a hard week, I deserve a treat.'

> 'Have a cig, I don't have much money for heaven's sake, I can't waste them.'

> 'Just finish the packet and then quit again.'

> 'A cigarette would be lovely now, go on, I really want to.'

> 'Just one won't hurt. I deserve a treat. It's the evening. Why shouldn't I just chill out and relax with a nice cigarette?'

> 'Plenty of people smoke, why am I making such a big deal about it?

> 'I'll just smoke occasionally - I've already proved I don't need to smoke all the time.'

> 'It's a Friday night, I deserve a treat after a hard week'.

I tried to watch television but couldn't settle. I tried to read a book but couldn't concentrate. I tried to cook a meal. But I didn't want a meal - I wanted a smoke! I started pacing the living room and all the while the voice in my head continued:

> 'Have a cig, things are hard for me at the moment, I need something to help me.'

'Have a cig, why should I make myself miserable?'

'Have a cig, it's only a cig for goodness sake, why am I making such a big deal out of it?'

'Have a cig, have a cig, have a cig…'

In the end I suddenly thought, 'This is ridiculous. If I want it that much, then I'm just going to have it. It's only a cigarette. It's not crack cocaine. Just have the damn thing.'

I took a cigarette out of the packet and was about to light up when it suddenly struck me, in a moment of total clarity, that the only reason I wanted this cigarette was to stop myself wanting it. The only reason I wanted this cigarette was that thoughts of it had consumed me for hours and I was sick of thinking about it. The only reason I wanted to smoke was to stop myself wanting to smoke, so I could actually think about or do something else that evening.

But the only reason I wanted to smoke was because I had smoked the last one. And smoking this one would guarantee the need to smoke the next one, and the one after that, and the one after that.

I realised that really wanting cigarettes is a horrible state to be in. Usually when I really want something it's because that thing is of genuine worth and value. But the desire to smoke is different. It is not a desire to do something worthwhile, or fun, or exciting, or pleasurable. It is just a desire to get rid of the desire! And it is a horrid feeling. The desire to go skiing is an exciting feeling. The desire to smoke is utterly negative.

All a cigarette does is get rid of the desire for a cigarette. But the only reason you have the desire is because of the last cigarette you smoked. Wanting to smoke feels horrible. Smoking stops you wanting to smoke for a little while. **And that is all it does.**

I sat there looking at the cigarette I was just about to light. I thought about how my evening had been dominated by thinking about smoking. I remembered how as a smoker my whole life had been dominated by the need and desire to smoke. Just a short week ago that desire was not there. And cigarettes were meaningless in my life. I realised I had a choice. Light up and keep the horrid feelings of needing and craving cigarettes alive, or ride out the feeling and get rid of it for good. I didn't light up. And I have never smoked again. Nor even wanted to.

All smoking does is stop you wanting to smoke... for a while.

The belief that smoking is relaxing is a fundamental misconception which keeps people stuck in the Nicotine Addiction Triangle for smoke after smoke after smoke. The key to successful quitting is to see through it.

Imagine the scene: you have had a dire day at work. Your boss has yelled at you. You have a thumping headache. It's pouring with rain, and you don't have an umbrella. Your car is in the garage, so you have to get a bus home. You sit on the bus soaking wet and cold. It gets caught in a dreadful traffic jam. When you get home you find you have lost your keys.

You sit on the doorstep in a terrible mood and light a cigarette or puff on a vape. Immediately you feel better. Your situation has not improved but at least you can have the pleasure of your habit, and this helps. Someone else in an identical situation would not have the benefit of that cigarette. So you are better off - right? Wrong!

Not only did you have to contend with the bad day at work, the hassle with the boss, the headache, the rain, traffic and lost keys. On top of all that misery, Nitch made an appearance too. Whining at you, demanding attention, insisting on being fed now as if you didn't have enough to worry about.

Think of Nitch as an annoying, persistent, ever-present little creature who won't take no for an answer. He hassles you and bugs you and irritates you until you give in and feed him - i.e. smoke or vape. As soon as you feed him, he shuts up and gives you some peace. So you experience relief - for a little while. But you are only relieving the stress that Nitch caused. Non- smokers in exactly the same position simply wouldn't have the extra hassle of having Nitch to deal with, on top of all their other worries.

Key Concept

> Smokers have all the real-life problems non-smokers have. On top of these they have Nitch.

I repeat: being a nicotine user is not relaxing. It is incredibly stressful. Even if nicotine was harmless, just being a slave to Nitch is enormously stressful. People must accept that their addiction means that they always have to think about cigarettes or vapes. Wherever they go they need to make sure their supply doesn't run out. If they are short of money they need to make other sacrifices.

In my smoking groups a number of smokers laugh at the ridiculous idea that they would ever find themselves running short of cigarettes. Some people go pale at the thought. This neatly illustrates how conscious and aware smokers are of the need to keep themselves permanently supplied with cigarettes. But I was the type of disorganised smoker who kept running out. And what a nightmare that was! Imagine you are out and suddenly discover you have only two cigarettes left. And you don't have much money. What are your options? Buy another drink, or buy some?

No contest! Unless you are confident of your scrounging abilities cigarettes win hands down. I once spent two hours standing on my own outside a cinema waiting for my friends. I had realised after meeting up with them that I couldn't afford both a packet of cigarettes and a cinema ticket and naturally the cigarettes won. I was only fifteen! I would never have dreamt that I could be hooked at that age. Cigarettes hook you fast.

Imagine you are on a camping trip and you get to your tent in the pouring rain to discover your cigarettes are drenched and have disintegrated, or your vape is out of battery. A weekend of no nicotine stretches before you. How far would you be prepared to walk in the rain to buy some more? How many total strangers would you be prepared to ask for a cigarette?

Now imagine how you would feel asking the same strangers for food or water. When it comes to satisfying Nitch, nicotine users are tireless and shameless. And this endless pandering to Nitch's desires is unbelievably stressful. The best thing about quitting for me wasn't the health gains, or the extra money. It was the sheer blissful relief of never having to think about Nitch again. It was an unbelievably precious sense of freedom. Once Nitch is dead, you can be completely free of him - providing, of course, that you no longer believe his propaganda.

Key Concept

> Killing Nitch frees you from the endless need to satisfy him.

'But I enjoy smoking!' I hear you cry impatiently. Okay, let's look at enjoyment.

Enjoyment

What do you enjoy about a cigarette or vape? The taste? The sensation of the smoke or vapour hitting the back of your throat? The deep breath in and the steady stream as you blow out? Beautifully crafted smoke rings? The feel of it in your hand - feeling so right there? The shiny colourful vapes up enticingly in the head shop window? I can still remember the tingle of anticipation I felt just seeing a shiny new packet, full of promises of comfort and luxury and indulgence.

Let's start with taste. Can you remember your first cigarette?

Unless you started later in life when you had already been victim to passive smoking for a while, or unless you had used tobacco in other forms before starting to smoke cigarettes, the first cigarette would not have relieved you of any tension. If you had never had any nicotine before, you would not yet have had the misfortune of meeting Nitch.

That first experience of smoking is what a cigarette is really like. Until Nitch sets up camp in your body, all cigarettes taste terrible.

At this early stage, smoking is largely image and nothing else. So kids will claim to enjoy their first few cigarettes. This is never true. Cigarettes are horrible when you are not addicted to nicotine. Even kids seem to know this and are on the lookout for anyone who is just pretending to inhale.

When I started smoking, the girls in my class who smoked would meet in McDonalds every Saturday. We would immediately light up. Anyone watching would have been able to witness the ludicrous spectacle of half a dozen fourteen-year-old girls taking pathetic little drags, saying things like, 'God I need this,' and trying desperately to leave the stub burning between drags so that they didn't have to smoke so much without anyone noticing.

We girls were deeply suspicious of anyone who might not really be inhaling. We would watch newcomers to the group like hawks, ready to pounce on them.

'You didn't inhale,' we would shout accusingly.

'I did, I did,' would come the plaintive cry.

'Prove it!' we would demand and the poor smoker would have to inhale, say a few words, then exhale. Only then would they have passed our stupid little test.

What was going on there? Here was a group of teenagers all doing something they secretly knew they hated, all deeply suspicious that other people might hate it too, and all utterly contemptuous of anyone if they showed evidence that they did hate it.

Once at the weekly McDonalds trip a new girl joined us. After we had smoked our obligatory B&H we stubbed them out with relief. To our horror the new girl took another cigarette out of the packet, then offered the pack around. Another one - no way! But image was all-important so we all dutifully lit up again. Afterwards I was sick on the bus home.

Those early cigarettes represent what cigarettes truly taste like, if you don't have nicotine addiction as a complicating factor. They taste disgusting. And cigarettes don't change!

Key Concept

Cigarettes taste disgusting - you just get used to it.

Addicted smokers 'develop a taste' for cigarettes because over time they come to associate smoking with relief. The only 'good' bit about smoking is relief from nicotine withdrawal. In fact, that is the only thing that matters at all. If someone gave you a cigarette that was identical in taste and smell to your normal cigarettes, but had no nicotine in it, it would give you no satisfaction. But the fact that your cigarettes do contain nicotine means that they do satisfy.

What about vapes? One of the most infuriatingly cynical things about vaping is the way in which colourful vapes in funky flavours specifically to overcome the fact that smokes are grim. This means that kids take up vaping younger, and some of the barriers to starting a nicotine dependency are removed. But flavour/taste is not the reason you vape. Lots of things smell nice and lots of people enjoy various smells/tastes. But no-one climbs walls in agitation because their aromatherapy oils have run out.

Key Concept

Vapes taste ok -but that is NOT why you like them!

It is crucial to successful quitting to recognise that the feelings of satisfaction arise from a misconception: this happens because people confuse relief with pleasure. Relief is the removal of something unpleasant (which makes you feel better afterwards). True pleasures add something to your life. And when you also consider that the unpleasantness that is removed by nicotine is also *caused* by nicotine, it becomes clear that there is no good reason to continue at all. Cigarettes and vapes are not enjoyable on their own. The genuine relief is no reason to carry on, because nicotine only relieves the misery it causes. The 'pleasure' of a nicotine hit is simply the relief of Nitch-whingeing.

The handling aspects are also irrelevant. They only seem pleasant or important because you have become conditioned to associate these actions with relief.

Which cigarettes or vapes do you 'enjoy' most? Most people find the cigarettes they smoke after a longish gap to be most satisfying. For example, first thing in the morning, a smoke after a meal, or the first one after you have been unable to puff for a while.

But all cigarettes and vapes are the same. This is so blindingly obvious but is rarely considered by smokers. They don't change just because it's after a meal. The difference is simply how much you need the nicotine.

The difference between pleasure and relief is shown in the following story.

Years ago when I still smoked I had the incredible opportunity to go to Spitsbergen in the High Arctic for nine weeks on a mountaineering trip. I knew I couldn't smoke when I was there, because we would be completely cut off from civilisation. I was very worried about how bad the first few days/weeks would be because I had experienced terrible withdrawal cravings in my many previous failed attempts at quitting. I never intended to quit completely at that time because I believed that the only way of coping on the utterly smokeless Arctic ice cap was to think about the glorious promise of the cigarettes to come when we got back to civilisation.

We all coped with bland, monotonous rehydrated food by dreaming endlessly about the gorgeous feast we would have in a few weeks' time, and I did exactly the same thing with cigarettes - picturing myself outside the tent, in a bar, on a mountain, dragging deeply and satisfyingly on a gorgeous Marlboro Red.

I was pleasantly surprised about how few withdrawal symptoms I had. At the time I didn't know that most withdrawal symptoms are caused by Nitch's propaganda, not by physical withdrawal. In the Arctic there was absolutely no option of smoking. Usually when you quit Nitch, comes up with endless excuses and justifications to make you start again. It is this constant commentary about whether you should/shouldn't smoke that is so stressful and exhausting. But if there is no possibility of smoking, then Nitch falls silent. He can't influence your decisions because there aren't any to be made.

Nevertheless, I was eagerly anticipating the pleasures of the first post-trip cigarette. My first truly powerful craving to smoke began as soon as the possibility of smoking became a reality. We had planned to be back in civilisation by noon, plenty of time before the shops shut. But the boat was delayed, and we didn't get back until nightfall. This was still a very remote settlement and nothing was open. Suddenly, having coped perfectly well with not smoking for over nine weeks, I found the prospect of one more night without cigarettes unbearable.

Another group of mountaineers was camped nearby so I asked them for a cigarette and, joy of joys, they had plenty. I lit up, inhaled deeply and … nothing. I felt a bit sick but I was expecting that because I hadn't smoked for ages. I also expected it to taste grim, because I never really liked the taste of cigarettes, but there was something hugely wrong with the cigarette that went beyond just not tasting very nice. It wasn't *satisfying*.

I now realise that it wasn't satisfying because I had absolutely no nicotine in my body which meant there was no dis-satisfaction to relieve. But at that time, I was bewildered, frustrated and deeply disappointed. 'The cigarette isn't working,' I said plaintively. 'There's something wrong with it.' Of course, there was nothing wrong with the cigarette. It was just that if you have no need of nicotine then cigarettes do not satisfy.

Unfortunately, I didn't know that then, and I decided the cigarette must have been stale and that I would buy a new pack the next day. Which I did. I still had a clear memory of what a smoke 'should' feel like, along with many memories of 'enjoyable' and 'satisfying' cigarettes, and I didn't know they were misconceptions. After three more 'useless' cigarettes that 'didn't work', I finally smoked one that felt the way they used to feel.

Lucky me - I had just resurrected Nitch and now could 'enjoy' cigarettes again. That misunderstanding cost me another year of smoking.

If you are still convinced that you smoke because you like the taste, think about what you would do if there were no brands that you liked on offer. When I was a smoker I hated menthol cigarettes. The mintiness affected the way the smoke felt on the back of my throat and just didn't feel right. But if there was nothing else available, would I smoke menthols or go without? Smoke menthols, obviously. Same goes for vapes. If you buy a new flavour of liquid and decide you don't like it, but your choice is either: a) don't vape, or b) puff on the flavour you don't like, what would you do?

Suck it up, of course. (Literally as well as metaphorically!) In fact, I've been known to smoke butts out of old ashtrays rather than go without cigarettes. And on one memorable occasion, I was pacing the house, unable to leave because I was babysitting and unable to find my cigarettes because my sister had nicked them. (I'd give my sister my house, but my cigarettes? You've got to be joking.)

I was frantically searching in pockets of old coats and in the depths of handbags. To my delight I found a cigarette. So it was a bit green and damp looking but, hey, a smoke is a smoke. Similarly, when a disposable vape dies, you go through old, dead vapes in drawers and pockets, puffing on them all in turn in the hope at least one of them will give you one final puff, even though they taste vile.

Manky cigs and dead vapes are not in the least tasty, but they certainly still satisfy. There is a big difference. Enjoyment is something extra you get from doing or having something nice. Smoking is simply the temporary relief of dissatisfaction and misery.

Leisure and social behaviours

Other smokes that people find most 'pleasurable' or 'enjoyable' are those they have when they are out socially, or when they are relaxing. In these situations, people are doing things that are genuinely pleasurable. They may be out with friends, or at a party, or unwinding after work. One of my favourite cigarettes was the one I had as soon as I got home from work. I had a whole ritual surrounding this precious cigarette. I would change into comfortable clothes, make a cup of tea, put on some relaxing music, then sit on the sofa, put my feet up and light up. If you pair something irrelevant with something nice repeatedly, the thing that you have paired with the pleasure becomes pleasurable in itself.

In the situation I have just described all the things I was doing were genuinely pleasurable and relaxing. The cigarette became associated with these pleasures till it seemed as if it was the cigarette itself that was the most important thing. If you always smoke or vape in situations when you are relaxing, drinking, socialising or unwinding, then the cigarettes/e-cigs becomeassociated with those pleasures, and you feel that they are a crucial part of them.

When you first quit, these situations feel odd, as if there is something missing. What the research has shown, however, is that if you break the link, the conditioning fades. You will therefore find that you enjoy the genuine pleasures of those situations as much as you ever did. We will look at this concept in more detail in the next chapter.

Enhancing enjoyment of other activities

Another reason why the belief that smoking makes good times even better is to do with Nitch, and how he behaves if you do not feed him. People often find that they cannot enjoy situations when they are not using nicotine. No matter how good their holiday is, it just would not be enjoyable without keeping Nitch happy.

So isn't that good evidence of the value of nicotine – it makes good times even better? No! This is another misconception. Another cost in disguise. People don't enjoy things **more** if they can smoke or vape, but they certainly enjoy them **less** if they can't. This is not the same thing! If you are keeping him supplied, Nitch will allow you to enjoy the rest of your holiday. But he won't add anything to it.

Nicotine is irrelevant when you are regularly topping it up. But when nicotine is not available or convenient, Nitch will make an awful fuss, prevent you from enjoying anything, or will insist that you suffer significant inconvenience to feed him.

I used to ski every year and a group of friends and I would stay in a hosted chalet. Smoking was not permitted in the chalet. One year there was only one smoker who had to stand outside in the freezing cold by himself every time Nitch needed feeding. So in the evenings we would all be sitting around by the lovely log fire, chatting, drinking red wine and playing cards, while he was shivering outside getting his nicotine fix. Smoking didn't add anything at all to his holiday. It just got in the way. (Isn't it funny how smokers in those sorts of situations will say, 'I like the fresh air', but when they quit they never feel the urge to experience sub-zero 'fresh air' in the middle of the night again?)

How much nicer it is not to have to think about Nitch, or worry about him, or pander to his endless demands.

In one of my groups a woman told me that her daughter had recently got married. As she sat in church watching her daughter's wedding ceremony, all she was thinking was, 'I hope they hurry up, because I really want a cigarette.' That was a perfect (though tragic) example of how cigarettes get in the way of enjoyment and destroy special occasions while adding absolutely nothing of value at all. And this is not a unique occurrence - quitting adviser Allen Carr admits to having had the same experience at his own daughter's wedding before he gave up.

Coping

'Okay, okay, maybe cigarettes are stressful and it's a pain to have to smoke all the time. But if I didn't smoke, I just couldn't function properly. I need to smoke to keep me focused at work.'

People will often say that smoking helps them concentrate. It keeps them sharp. It adds an edge of creativity. If you are stuck at work, what better way to unstick yourself than to have a puff. Afterwards solutions present themselves and you can think more clearly.

Nonsense! This is just another cost cunningly disguised as a benefit.

In the same way that nicotine makes you stressed while pretending to be helping you feel less stressed, it also destroys your ability to concentrate while pretending to improve it. Imagine trying to concentrate on your job with a tantrumming toddler demanding sweets from you. Nitch operates the same way. And he is tremendously distracting. When he wants feeding he will not let it rest. He cannot take no for an answer. And he won't leave you alone till you give in and feed him. Just like the toddler he then pipes down, so you can heave a sigh of relief and get on with some work ... till next time.

But again, instead of blaming nicotine for creating such a distraction, you assume that the smoke is actually giving your concentration a boost. This is another example of Nitch's power over you. He manages to distract you and impair your concentration day in and day out, while at the same time making you believe that cigarettes or vapes (his lifeline) are helpful to you.

Habit

Some people will say they know cigarettes don't do anything for them. They feel that smoking is 'just a habit', but one they can't seem to break.

People tend to smoke or vape at the same times and in the same places. When you quit it feels harder to enjoy those situations. Something feels missing. This is an important point that needs to be addressed - because habit is the third corner of our Nicotine Addiction Triangle. Chapter 8 discusses this.

Addiction

'Okay, so maybe all I'm doing is feeding an addiction. Knowing that doesn't make it any easier to stop. After all, beating addiction is incredibly difficult. And smoking is one of the hardest of them all.'

It is certainly true that nicotine is highly addictive. But this does not mean that you can't escape. Addiction is poorly understood and there are many misconceptions about addicts, such as 'once an addict always an addict'. These misconceptions developed because of the great difficulty some people have in giving up smoking. Other evidence shows that some people who do stop smoking still crave cigarettes. You may meet people who tell you that they quit ten years ago and still could 'murder a cigarette'. Other people will tell you that despite long-term success in quitting, they still feel as if they are addicts: 'If I had one I'd go straight back to twenty a day.'

You yourself may have quit for months and years before, but nonetheless felt drawn to smoking and had to use constant willpower to stay off the vape or cigarettes, before eventually relapsing.

Despite all this, it is still untrue to say that people cannot be totally free. It is true that some people quit and continue to crave cigarettes long after all nicotine has disappeared from their bodies. However, research into ex-smokers also shows that many of them do not continue to crave. Many look back on their smoking with bafflement - they remember how important cigarettes seemed at the time, but they can't for the life of them figure out why. They no longer relate to smoking. They often find the smell offensive and they have no idea what on earth made them do it for so long. They get annoyed by huge vape clouds from people in the street. These are not people who are constantly having to exert willpower. They are truly free from smoking, and cigarettes/vapes are now completely unimportant in their lives.

Okay, you might say, all that shows is that some people are lucky enough not to have addictive personalities. But the research is more complicated and interesting than that: the **same** smoker can sometimes quit and never miss cigarettes afterwards, and yet sometimes quit and find themselves suffering terrible cravings.

So how come they started smoking again if they didn't miss smoking at all? Good question - I'm glad you're paying attention.

The answer is simply that there are many pitfalls that trap unwary non-smokers or ex-smokers. People who are totally free can still get hooked again. It is incredibly common for a person to say 'I quit smoking for 2 years about 3 years ago and I was totally fine. But then I had one at a party and ended up smoking again, and now I can't even imagine life without it. And when I try to quit again I am climbing the walls'.

Chapter 13 is devoted to the important issue of preventing a relapse once you have managed to get yourself free. For now, all you need to know is that you can quit and be totally free and not miss cigarettes or vapes at all, or you can quit and still not be free but continue to miss and crave cigarettes or e-cigs. And the same person can experience both types of quitting. The message therefore is that there is nothing inherent in a person's brain or personality that makes it impossible to quit and be free. Everyone can be free. Including you.

Let's take a closer look at addiction and its different definitions. People claim to be addicted to almost anything - chocolate or sex for example. One definition of addiction is that there is a change in your body when you withdraw from a substance. Heroin is a good example of that. Nicotine is also an example of a substance that changes the way you feel when it leaves your system. The problem with nicotine is that the nature of the withdrawal is far from understood and it varies dramatically from person to person, and even in the same person on different occasions. Studies of withdrawal show that the actual physical changes in people's bodies are not what they complain about. Indeed, many people don't even notice these physical changes. What people do complain about are emotional states like grouchiness or irritability.

People can experience a similar sort of grouchiness or irritability when they go without things that are not physically addictive, as compulsive gamblers do, for example. Part of withdrawal is clearly psychological.

Some people use a descriptive definition of addiction. They describe behaviours and feelings that people have towards certain substances or activities to decide if a person is addicted to a particular substance or activity or not. The central feature of any addiction is so-called compulsive use. This means that people will go to great lengths to obtain the substance or continue the activity, and that they experience distress without it. The addiction label does not explain why a person behaves compulsively. It simply describes what people do and feel.

This definition of addiction fits nicotine addicts, who make great efforts to get nicotine and feel stressed, anxious or panicky without it. But describing something as addictive still does not *explain* it. The questions you need to ask yourself are:

- *Why* do I have a compulsive need to smoke or vape?

- *Why* will I go to such ridiculous lengths to get a cigarette or e-cig?

- *Why* am I so miserable without them?

The answer can again be found in our little villain, Nitch. Nitch can physically make you feel stressed all the time by inducing withdrawal symptoms. As we have seen, these lead to anxiety, which we reduce by feeding Nitch again.

But this happens in our survival brain, and we are completely unaware of it. So we need to find another reason. Which brings us onto Nitch's second weapon: propaganda. This makes us believe that we need cigarettes in order to be relaxed or confident, sociable, good at our job - or simply to function. It is not a physical state but an emotional one.

These beliefs make quitting much harder. Added to the real anxiety of nicotine withdrawal, you have the emotional turmoil of imagining life without your precious cigarettes or e-cigs.

A woman in one of my groups started using the drug bupropion (Zyban) to help her quit (more on this later). She was to take one tablet a day for six days while continuing to smoke. From day seven, she was to take two tablets a day while still smoking. On day eleven she was to quit smoking. Her 'withdrawal symptoms' began on day nine - while she was still smoking. By the end of day ten they were so bad that she didn't dare take her evening tablet. She knew that she was meant to stop the following day, and this filled her with so much panic that she stopped using the drugs altogether, and abandoned the quit attempt before it even began. Her misery was not about withdrawal. It was about dread and panic at the thought of withdrawal.

Another person in the group returned for his follow-up and was deeply unhappy because he had failed to stop.

'I just couldn't do it,' he said.

'What went wrong?' I asked. 'What made it so difficult to stop?'

'The withdrawal symptoms', he replied.

'At what point did you give in to the withdrawal symptoms and smoke?'

'As soon as I woke up.'

This man went on to describe how terrible he felt as soon as he woke up, and how desperately he was craving cigarettes. These awful feelings had nothing at all to do with physical withdrawal symptoms. If he hadn't been quitting he would have felt fine on waking, even though he would have been experiencing exactly the same amount of physical withdrawal.

Chapter summary

- Cigarettes appear to relax you, because they take away the anxiety they cause - for a while.

- Vapes appear satisfying because they create dissatisfaction then take it away again - for a while.

- Cigarettes appear to help you enjoy yourself because Nitch makes you miserable if you don't feed him.

- Vapes appear to help you concentrate because they distract you, then restore your concentration - for a while.

- Seeing through Nitch's propaganda is an important part of quitting.

Read the following account by a man talking about his quit attempt to understand what can go wrong in quit attempts if you haven't understood Nitch's dirty tricks.

"I tried to quit last week but it was a bad time at work. On quit date I was having a really difficult day. My boss was getting at me, and I was under a lot of pressure. I really needed to focus and concentrate on this big project and smoking helps me with that. So, I decided after a terrible morning to give up the quit attempt till the weekend when I was not under so much pressure.

Saturday morning was my next attempt. It was going okay till about ten o'clock when my grandchildren came over. I love them dearly but they are a real handful and frankly their behaviour was pretty terrible. Well, I couldn't cope with them at all. They were really winding me up and I could feel that I would lose my temper with them. So I went and bought a packet and they helped me to cope with the kids. Actually smoking really does stop me being so irritable. I deal with everything much better when I can have a smoke, so I am worried about the impact quitting will have on my family.

Anyway, I'd blown it for Saturday so I thought I'd try Sunday. It was fine till the afternoon when I went to play golf with some friends. They all smoke and were pretty dismissive of my attempt to quit, telling me what a waste of time that was, and warning me of the misery ahead. So that didn't help much. After the game we were in the beer garden having a cold lager, and they offered me a cigarette. Well, I couldn't relax and have a good time without one and after a long and difficult week at work I felt I deserved to be able to unwind.

I started thinking that I'd much rather be relaxed and happy even if that meant damaging my health. Health is important, of course, but it's not everything. I don't want to be a miserable old sod for the rest of my days. I felt tired of punishing myself and thought I needed and deserved to be able to relax with my friends. Smoking helps me do that. So I had a few.

All in all, when I think back on how the week has gone, I reckon that despite the costs and risks, I'd rather just keep smoking for the moment. Maybe when I retire next year I'll give it another go."

Can you identify the fundamental misconception in this account? How often?

The following page discusses some of the errors he is making. Try to identify some of them yourself before you read on, return to Chapter 6 to refresh your memory. If you can spot this in other people, you are much more likely to notice it in yourself.

Let's look at the account again:

I tried to quit last week but it was a bad time at work. On quit date I was having a really difficult day. My boss was getting at me and I was under a lot of pressure. I really needed to focus and concentrate on this big project and smoking helps me with that.

This is an example of the fundamental misconception. The belief is that smoking helps concentration. The smoker believes that the pressure of work is to blame for the problems in concentrating, and the cigarette helps him to sharpen up. In reality the drop in nicotine is to blame for the problems in concentrating, and having a cigarette relieves this distraction.

So I decided after a terrible morning to give up the quit attempt till the weekend when I was not under so much pressure. Saturday morning was my next attempt. It was going okay till about ten o'clock when my grandchildren came over. I love them dearly but they are a real handful and frankly their behaviour was pretty terrible. Well, I couldn't cope with them at all. They were really winding me up and I could feel that I would lose my temper with them. So I went and bought a packet and they helped me to cope with the kids. Actually smoking really does stop me being so irritable.

Here again the smoker is being tricked by the fundamental misconception. He is blaming his grandchildren for the increase in his irritability. They are winding him up. However, once he has had a smoke, the same behaviours no longer wind him up. Why not? Because it wasn't them at all that were winding him up. Rather, the drop in nicotine levels was causing irritability, and the cigarette relieved that irritability. Nitch was annoying him, not his grandchildren. The man is, however, blaming the children instead of Nitch for his tension. So he believes cigarettes are actually helpful to him rather than being the cause of his problems.

I deal with everything much better when I can have a smoke, so I am worried about the impact quitting will have on my family.

The fundamental misconception described above leads him to a general conclusion about the impact of smoking on his relationships. This is an example of over-generalisation. The generalisation is that smoking helps. In reality, smoking makes him stressed and irritable. The belief that smoking helps people with irritability is a common excuse for carrying on smoking. Parents say they deal with their children better after a smoke. However, this is simply because being a nicotine addict makes you tense and irritable. A cigarette temporarily relieves that problem, but the smoker is still more tense and irritable overall.

Anyway, I'd blown it for Saturday so I thought I'd try Sunday. It was fine till the afternoon when I went to play golf with some friends. They all smoke and were pretty dismissive of my attempt to quit, telling me what a waste of time that was, and warning me of the misery ahead.

This is an example of sabotage, common among smokers whose friends/family are quitting. This is further discussed later in the book.

So that didn't help much. After the game we were in the beer garden having a cold lager, and they offered me a cigarette. Well I couldn't relax and have a good time without one.

This is another example of the fundamental misconception. The man believes that smoking is pleasurable and relaxing. In reality, if you are a nicotine addict, it is not possible to be totally relaxed without a cigarette because nicotine withdrawal is stressful. The man is unable to relax because he is experiencing nicotine withdrawal. Smoking temporarily removes that barrier to relaxation.

Smoking because you cannot relax unless you are smoking is a very different thing from smoking because smoking is relaxing. The latter is the fundamental misconception which implies a genuine beneficial effect of smoking - pleasure and relaxation. The former, on the other hand, is similar to a person with fleas! Unless you relieve the itching, you will not have a good time. But the flea bites are not actually helping you, even though scratching them provides relief. Looking at it like that shows how difficult it is ever to relax if you are a smoker.

Being miserable without smokes does not mean smoking makes you happy.

I started thinking that I'd much rather be relaxed and happy even if that meant damaging my health. Health is important, of course, but it's not everything. I don't want to be a miserable old sod for the rest of my days. I felt tired of punishing myself and thought I needed and deserved to be able to relax with my friends.

Again, the specific fundamental misconception has led to a general belief on the importance of smoking in this man's life.

Smoking helps me do that. So I had a few. All in all, when I think back on how the week has gone, I reckon that despite the costs and risks, I'd rather just keep smoking for the moment. Maybe when I retire next year I'll give it another go.

This man's unhappy experiences of quitting have led him to a decision to continue smoking. However, his conclusions are based on distorted thinking. To quit, he needs to change his perceptions of his experiences of smoking. That is the aim of this book.

Worksheet

Costs in diguise

Finish each of these sentences from the choices presented below.

NOT ENJOYMENT BUT ....

NOT IMPROVED CONCENTRATION BUT ....

....

NOT RELAXATION BUT ....

NOT PLEASURE BUT ....

NOT FREE CHOICE BUT ....

Choose from the following:
- distraction then partial relief
- addiction
- conditioning
- inability to have fun without smoking
- stress then partial relief of stress

Worksheet

Now add some of your own:

NOT ....

BUT ....

NOT ....

BUT ....

NOT ....

BUT ....

NOT ....

BUT ....

Chapter 8:
Habit

Most people smoke or vape at certain times and places throughout the day. They will automatically puff in certain situations, without necessarily even being aware of it. When people quit, they often find that they are coping okay when they are in unfamiliar places, or places where they rarely took in nicotine, but that as soon as they get to a 'smoking' situation the cravings suddenly intensify. Again, this is evidence that withdrawal symptoms are not just physical. Your nicotine levels have not plummeted because you have walked into a beer garden or out of the office.

Some people say smoking or vaping is 'just a habit' because they notice that they can stop for long periods in some situations, but light up automatically in others.

Breaking the habit seems very difficult, and people often worry that they will never enjoy many of the things they used to enjoy, because cigarettes or vapes are so strongly associated with them.

Cravings can also be triggered when people see or smell cigarettes or vapes, for example catching sight of a cigarette kiosk at the supermarket, walking past the Duty-Free Shop at an airport or smelling the vapour as someone walks past.

Why should the sight of cigarettes or certain places trigger cravings in someone who was not even thinking about nicotine before?

To overcome these potential problems, we need to understand why cravings are triggered.

What we call 'habit' is called conditioning in psychology. Many years ago, a scientist named Pavlov described classical conditioning. He noticed that dogs tended to produce saliva when they were presented with food. This salivation was called the unconditioned response, meaning that it was a natural response to the smell and sight of food.

What Pavlov did next was to ring a bell whenever he fed the dogs. This meant that the dogs salivated whenever they saw or smelled food, and they also salivated when they heard a bell. The bell was irrelevant, but the dogs salivated when they heard it, because they always heard it at the same time as they were given food.

Next Pavlov rang the bell, without offering the dogs any food. The dogs began to salivate as soon as they heard the bell. This was called the conditioned response. There is no reason why a dog should salivate when it hears a bell, but in this instance the dogs had learnt to associate the bell with food.

Conditioning is now clearly understood as the process by which something irrelevant takes on meaning by being paired with something that is meaningful. This has several implications for smoking. The taste, smell and sensations of your chosen nicotine delivery system are irrelevant. You just want the drug because nicotine provides relief. But every time you experience satisfaction and relief of nicotine withdrawal, lots of other stimuli are present at the same time. The handling, the taste and smell, the sensation of smoke or vapour entering your lungs are all present every time you get relief from nicotine withdrawal. So you start to associate other aspects of smoking with the relief. You therefore start to believe that these things on their own are important. They are not. You have just been programmed or *conditioned* to see them as important.

Key Concept

> Nicotine users have been conditioned to think of taste, sensation and handling as satisfying because they associate these things with relief of nicotine withdrawal.

When people quit, they miss all these associated elements. They miss the handling aspects, the smell and taste, and the rituals involved.

We also become conditioned to see smoking or vaping as pleasurable and relaxing because we generally smoke in pleasurable and relaxing situations, so nicotine becomes associated with social occasions, friends, going out, and breaks from work.

If you smoke whenever you are in relaxing situations, you gradually start to associate those pleasant feelings with smoking. This is a conditioned response. Smoking is not the relaxing bit about coming home from work, putting your feet up and having a cup of tea, but it becomes associated with those things, and takes on their qualities.

So just like the dog salivating over something irrelevant (a bell) because it is associated with something relevant (food), you relax or feel good over something irrelevant (a cigarette) because it is associated with something relevant (relaxation, leisure, sociability).

Once this conditioned response has developed, you will find that those situations trigger thoughts of smoking. If you are trying to quit, those situations may trigger cravings.

How do you escape from this angle of the Nicotine Addiction Triangle? Pavlov took his experiments a little further. What he found was that when you broke the link between the stimulus (the bell) and the thing it was associated with (the food), the dogs gradually stopped associating the bell with food. The bell lost its power. This process was called extinction.

What this means for smoking is that when you stop smoking, all those situations where you used to smoke feel weird at first. When you quit you will obviously continue to see and smell cigarettes and vapes. In situations where you have always vaped in the past, you will feel you are missing out, because you will still have some positive associations.

But as long as you don't smoke, the association between the sight and smell of a cigarette, and relief or satisfaction will fade away. In addition, the association between pleasure, sociability, relaxation and friendship will also fade away, and the link between smoking and those situations will gradually be extinguished.

Once this has happened, you will be able to enjoy the genuinely relaxing aspects of life as much as ever before, without feeling you are missing out on anything. In fact, you will be able to enjoy them more than ever before because you won't have the hassle of dealing with Nitch whenever you are out. You will never again experience the awful and irritating twitchiness and distractibility that smokers suffer so often. Unable to focus on enjoying being out with your friends because you need to keep leaving to go outside for a puff.

The only exception to this is when your beliefs about smoking are still distorted. If you firmly believe that there is something wonderful about handling a cigarette or vape, that belief will lead you to crave them long after the conditioned response has broken down. People who fall into this trap have a strong memory of how satisfying using nicotine felt, and they keep this memory alive and well.

These false memories make quitting endless - you are free of nicotine but Nitch is still in your head nagging you to smoke. Many people in this situation eventually get fed up with never feeling free of smoking, and are at very high risk of relapse. That is why you need to tackle all three angles of the Nicotine Addiction Triangle to be completely free.

One crucial part of Pavlov's work was to notice what happened if you broke the link between the bell and the food most of the time, but paired the two together occasionally. This is the equivalent of not vaping or smoking most of the time, but having the odd puff in certain situations. Pavlov found that if you sometimes paired two things together, then extinction did **not** take place. If the food was occasionally still paired with a bell, the dogs would continue to get very excited and drool when they heard a bell.

In order to conquer this habit you need to break the links **completely**. If you quit totally, then the links disappear, and your problems will be over. If you 'cheat' occasionally, then the links will not disappear: you will still 'drool' and will never be completely free.

You will still associate smoking with pleasure and relaxation long after you have 'quit'. This is another reason why social smoking is very difficult to sustain, and miserable even if you can do it. Social smokers never break free of the third angle. In fact they never truly break free of any of the angles: they are still addicted to nicotine, or they become regularly re-addicted if they smoke very occasionally; they still hold positive beliefs about smoking and vaping - or why would they bother with it at all; and they still have a conditioned response. Do not make life harder for yourself! Quitting must mean quitting completely.

Key Concept

If you stop smoking the conditioning vanishes. If you smoke occasionally it doesn't.

To overcome the conditioned response all you need to do is stop pairing cigarettes or vapes with any pleasurable situation. This will happen automatically if you quit. Simply being aware of what is happening when cravings are triggered can really help. However, if you want to reduce the cravings you experience, then you can take some practical steps to limit the conditioned response:

Tips to help you break the conditioned response

- Increase your self-awareness of triggers and urges. Bring conscious awareness to your smoking behaviours.

- Interrupt habits by smoking in the opposite hand, changing routines etc.

- Move furniture around your living room and stop smoking in your 'smoking chair' or anywhere else where smoking is common. Prior to quitting, when you smoke or vape, treat it as it is - a functional need - and only smoke standing up and/or in places that have no other significance and are not generally associated with relaxation.

- Change the order in which you do things.

These all help to break the link between specific situations and using nicotine. This might seem strange, but even simple changes like these can make a big difference.

- Use competing behaviours to manage urges: E.g. slowly sip ice cold water. Have a hand massage. File and paint nails. Play a hand-held game on your phone. Practice a musical instrument.

- Learn to relax with the relaxation and meditation

downloads. We are more reactive and more negative when we are physically tense.

Do not confuse genuine pleasures with the conditioned response. If something is pleasurable in its own right, do it anyway. You may not enjoy it at first because it reminds you that you are not smoking or vaping, but if you persist, then enjoyment of the activity comes back, while the link with nicotine disappears.

Be patient. It may take a while before not using nicotine in any way feels comfortable and familiar.

Don't panic if cravings are unexpectedly triggered a long time after quitting. This can and will happen occasionally. If there are certain situations in which you always used to smoke, but you have not revisited them for a long time, the desire to smoke may be triggered the first time you are in that situation again.

This happened to me. I used to live in London and got the tube home from work every day. As I left the station I would light up and smoke my first post-work cigarette while I walked the rest of the way home. I then moved out of London, and years later stopped smoking. Two years after quitting, I returned to London to visit friends. I had not been back to that part of the city since quitting smoking. I got out at my old tube station, started walking down the same street and automatically reached into my jacket pocket for my cigarettes!

Fortunately, I did not panic. I realised that the link between this specific street and smoking had not been extinguished because I had not been back, and that the old behaviour was being triggered - the way a smell can send you back in time. I did not smoke, and the next time I walked down the street the link was no longer there.

Remember that a craving is a feeling not a command. Accept it. It won't last long and, as long as you don't smoke, it will eventually disappear forever.

Chapter summary

- If things are paired together often enough, they become strongly associated with each other. This is called conditioning.

- We are conditioned to see things like taste, sensations, the handling aspects, or seeing bars in a shop as satisfying because they all become associated with relief of nicotine withdrawal.

- We are also conditioned to see cigarettes and vapes as relaxing because we smoke in relaxing and sociable places.

- If you break the link between nicotine and these places, the conditioned response disappears.

- If you occasionally vape or smoke the link remains.

- This means that the odd puff here or there actually makes quitting much harder.

Chapter 9:
Killing Nitch -
Understanding Withdrawal

We have learnt about the three angles of the Nicotine Addiction Triangle: physical addiction, psychological dependence and habit. To summarise:

Angle 1: Addiction

If you use nicotine you will frequently experience nicotine withdrawal. This will cause anxiety which is interpreted by your subconscious mind as danger. You will feel compelled to reduce this anxiety by doing whatever worked best last time - which will always be smoking or vaping. When you replace the missing nicotine your anxiety will drop, and so nicotine use is reinforced. You have no idea that this is happening to you. This is Nitch's first weapon - anxiety. Nitch feeds on nicotine and he makes you anxious when nicotine is running low.

The process is a vicious cycle:

- The more addicted you get, the more anxiety you have.

- The more anxiety you have, the more relief you experience when you replace the nicotine.

- The more relief you experience, the more powerful the drive to reduce anxiety by using nicotine becomes.

- The more powerful the drive to reduce anxiety with nicotine becomes, the more you smoke or vape.

- The more you smoke, the more addicted you get.

Angle 2: Psychological dependence

You have no idea what is happening in angle 1. You may understand this intellectually, but you do not 'get' this at an emotional level. You don't understand the extraordinarily strong drive to do something that seems to not even do much for you, and that has serious health impacts. So you find it hard to explain your feelings and behaviours, and you enter a state of cognitive dissonance.

This is psychologically very uncomfortable, so you search for an alternative explanation for your behaviour, while at the same time downplaying your fears. This gives rise to psychological dependence. This is Nitch's second weapon - propaganda. Nitch needs you to feed him, so he fills your head with rubbish. You listen to this nonsense because you are actively looking for an explanation.

This is another vicious cycle:

- The more the costs mount up, the more cognitive dissonance you experience.

- The more cognitive dissonance you experience, the more you downplay fears and elevate benefits.

- The more you downplay fears and elevate benefits, the more you vape or smoke.

- The more you vape or smoke, the more the costs mount up.

Angle 3: Habit

You tend to smoke in the same places and at the same times. This means that you start to associate smoking with the genuine pleasures or benefits of those situations, such as a night out or a work break. This process is called conditioning (or habit) and triggers powerful desires to puff in certain places. These pleasure associations make psychological dependence more powerful because vaping and smoking will start to take on the qualities inherent in those situations.

Habit is a major reason why people relapse in 'high-risk situations'. They may be fine most of the time, but can still experience cravings if they go somewhere they always used to smoke. If you understand what is happening, it is much easier to ride out the craving and break the links between those situations and relapses.

The two types of withdrawal

To overcome nicotine addiction, you need to cut off Nitch's nicotine supply - and kill him! So you have to go through nicotine withdrawal. Nicotine withdrawal symptoms are feelings of edginess, tension, irritability or anxiety. Think back to when you last really needed a smoke or vape. Well, that edgy feeling is nicotine withdrawal. It is quite mild on its own, which is why most people can spend twelve hours on a long-haul flight and cope perfectly well without smoking. Nitch does not waste his breath peddling propaganda because you can't smoke. And there is no association with puffs and flights, so the habit angle is missing too. And withdrawal – alone - is manageable.

The vagueness and mildness of the symptoms is, ironically, what makes the drive for nicotine so difficult to understand. There are no euphoric effects that you have to give up, and there are no strong physical withdrawal symptoms to overcome. People are aware that they feel powerfully driven to smoke or vape, but they don't know why, and the strength of the compulsion seems totally out of proportion to what people get in return.

This leads people to search for alternative explanations for their habit, so the second process that occurs for all addicts is psychological dependence. Addicts come to believe that they need their drug, and that they cannot cope without it. Together these two processes form a formidable barrier to quitting. The relative importance of each is different for all drugs, but thoughts, beliefs and attitudes are crucial in all addictions. Even an addiction like heroin, which looks mostly physical, is in fact largely psychological. This is why people go back to the drug even after detox. Such people are no longer physically dependent, but they still feel they need the drug.

The power of psychological processes is even more apparent for those addictions that are not physical at all, such as food, sex or gambling. Compulsive gamblers, for example, are not physically dependent, but they still experience intense physical symptoms when deprived of their 'fix'.

'Withdrawal' symptoms are a combination of physical withdrawal, caused by reductions in levels of nicotine in the bloodstream, and psychological withdrawal, caused by your beliefs and attitudes. This leads to lots of confusion about nicotine withdrawal. All smokers experience it, but no one experiences it in exactly the same way as anyone else. Physical withdrawal involves your body ridding itself of the nicotine on which it has become dependent. This process kills Nitch, and his death throes can be felt by the person he lives in. Psychological withdrawal is a powerful process caused by feelings of loss, fear, deprivation, misery and stress. This is where Nitch's propaganda machine is at its most effective.

Key Concept

Nicotine withdrawal is a combination of physical withdrawal and psychological withdrawal.

Nitch's running commentary, aimed at keeping you feeding him, makes quitting seem overwhelmingly difficult, and leaves people feeling anxious and miserable at the thought of giving up. It is important to remember that at this stage these thoughts are just that - thoughts. They have no external reality. They are not real experiences.

Key Concept

Thoughts are just thoughts. They do not have external reality.

It is the thoughts themselves that give rise to anxiety and misery. It is not quitting that does this, since the anxiety and misery develop before you even quit. The way you think is making you feel terrible. If you change the way you think, you will also change how you feel, and how you experience quitting.

To illustrate how thinking affects how you experience quitting, think about times when smoking or vaping are impossible. If there is no possibility of using nicotine, then Nitch falls silent. He can't influence your decisions because there aren't any to be made. This is why – against all expectations – people could cope on long-haul flights after smoking was banned.

Remember my account of the trip to the Arctic. I went from thirty a day to zero overnight and the withdrawal symptoms I experienced were nowhere near as bad as I had expected. And nothing like the terrible symptoms I had when I was trying to quit in the past. This didn't make much sense at the time but now I realise that in the Arctic all I experienced was physical withdrawal, and that the misery I went through in other attempts to give up was mostly Nitch driving me round the bend with his endless doom and gloom about the tragedy of a smoke-free life.

If you no longer believe in Nitch's propaganda, or if you are in a place where smoking is totally impossible, then the second aspect of withdrawal is not experienced.

If people believe they want and need cigarettes or e-cigs, then the mild tension from withdrawal escalates to climbing the walls in desperation. The mild tension triggers the 'I need this' belief, which causes anxiety, which in turn strengthens that belief, and intensifies the anxiety. Beliefs will lead to fear and therefore present a barrier to quitting. This fear and misery confirms your belief that you need your fix, and a vicious cycle develops. The more miserable you feel, the more you believe that you cannot live without vaping or smoking. And the more you believe that you cannot live without those, then the more misery and fear you feel.

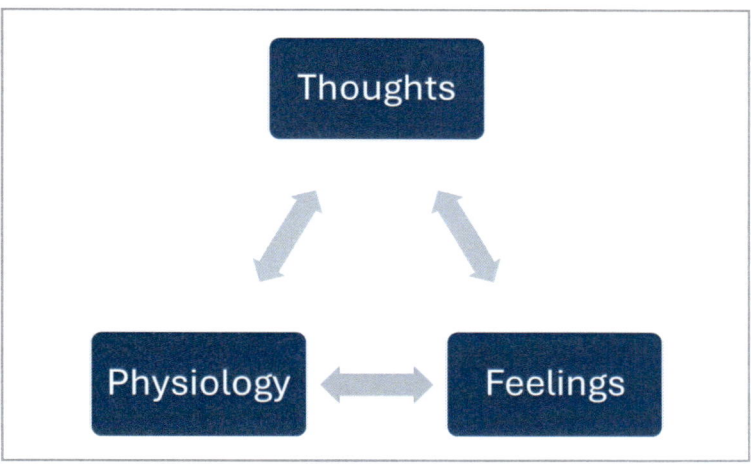

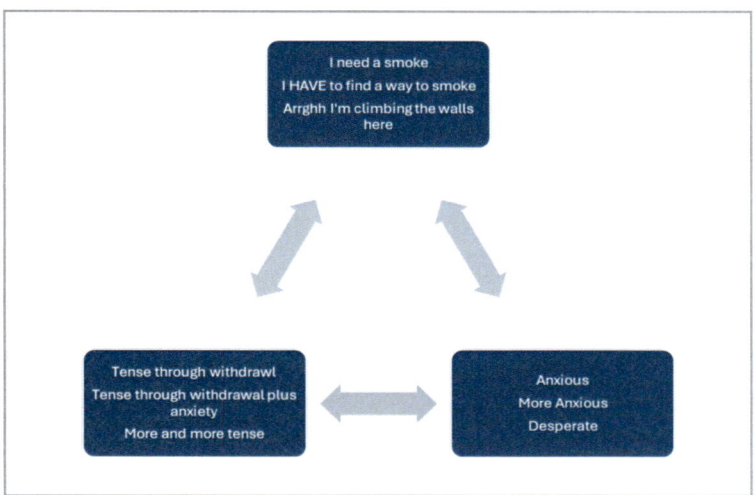

Eventually the person will smoke, and everything calms down. The conclusion then is 'I can't cope without it'. In this way, the misery and fear become a self-fulfilling prophecy, and people do feel wretched and miserable if they stop smoking. If you change your thinking, then you will have a different experience of quitting, even though the external reality is the same.

Key Concept

Changing the way you think, changes the way you feel.

Most people know that heroin is addictive and that if you quit you go 'cold turkey'. This is viewed by heroin users and non-users alike as a terrible ordeal. When servicemen were in Vietnam many thousands of them began to use heroin regularly to numb themselves from the horrors of war. Naturally they all got addicted and it was widely believed that this addiction was going to be a serious problem when the soldiers returned home. Against all expectations, most of the men gave up heroin easily and permanently as soon as they returned. [1] This can be explained in terms of the two types of withdrawal. The men knew perfectly well why they were using heroin in Vietnam. They did not feel stupid about it as they saw it as a necessary shield against the horror they were regularly subjected to. Because they had genuine reasons for using heroin they were not susceptible to the sort of Nitch-driven justifications that smokers use. So, when they got home the only problem was the physical withdrawal from heroin and, although this is unpleasant, on its own it was manageable.

Think about your own experiences of withdrawal. Most smokers start craving as they have their final puff. This is before Nitch has even begun to whimper. Conversely, many people can go for hours and hours in some situations, without any nicotine. If your mental state is right for quitting, withdrawal is not a problem.

Key Concept

> Most withdrawal symptoms are psychological.

This means you must free yourself from **both** processes. You need to overcome the physical dependence by cutting off the supply of nicotine and therefore killing Nitch. And you have to change the way you think about your habit, so that you no longer remain psychologically hooked. Many quit attempts focus on getting over the physical dependence. The problem is that people who are physically free but psychologically hooked do not feel free. They feel deprived and miserable. They may even still experience physical cravings, which are no less real to the poor sufferer just because they originate in their head.

You may meet people who quit years and years ago but still experience cravings. This observation has led many people, including some healthcare professionals, to believe that you can never truly overcome an addiction. Instead, people need to learn to live with being 'in recovery' forever. While it is true that some people never seem to get over it, others clearly do. The important question therefore is what is the difference between ex-addicts who feel totally free, and those who still feel trapped?

The answer is that the addicts who still feel trapped have not changed their internal scripts about the drug. They have only won half the war. Those who feel totally free have freed themselves from physical and psychological dependence.

Key Concept

> People who quit a long time ago and still miss cigarettes only freed themselves from nicotine addiction, not from psychological dependence. They only did half the job!

Freeing yourself from physical dependence means cutting off the supply of the drug, allowing it to leave your body and allowing your body to readapt to life without the drug. There are products such as various types of Nicotine Replacement Therapy (NRT) or the drugs bupropion (Zyban) and Varenicline (Champix) that can help you.

However, freeing yourself from physical addiction is not enough on its own. You also need to free yourself from psychological dependence, and you need to overcome the habit of smoking.

The next three chapters deal with each of these in turn.

Chapter Summary

- Quitting smoking involves tackling all three angles of the Nicotine Addiction Triangle.

- Angle 1 is nicotine addiction, which you can think of as Nitch making you anxious whenever his nicotine levels drop.

- Angle 2 is psychological dependence, which arises because of the positive beliefs you have about smoking or vaping. This can be seen as Nitch's propaganda.

- Angle 3 is habit. Habit or conditioning refers to the way in which you have gradually come to associate smoking or vaping with pleasure, relaxation or reduced stress. Nitch will use this conditioning as part of his propaganda machine.

- Withdrawal is a combination of physical and psychological withdrawal.

- If you deal with all three angles of the Nicotine Addiction Triangle then you will overcome both types of withdrawal.

Chapter 10: Overcoming Nicotine Addiction

It may help to reflect on the fact that nicotine withdrawal is mild. But never-the-less, we are powerfully motivated to reduce the anxiety of withdrawal, and so anything that helps take the edge off can help you quit.

We can approach this in 2 ways:

1) Manage your own physiology through relaxation, meditation and self-hypnosis.

2) Use products to address physical withdrawal.

Relaxation & Meditation

When smoking cessation advisors suggest that you learn relaxation techniques, the implication is that smoking is relaxing, so when you stop you need an alternative. As we have seen, this is totally untrue. However, learning to relax can help deal with the period of nicotine withdrawal. Learning effective ways to relax can benefit everyone, smoker or non-smoker. Smokers are, as a group, more stressed than non-smokers, because nicotine activates your Fight/Flight system – not to mention all the stress and hassle they cause indirectly. Learning deep relaxation skills will be very helpful to all smokers, to counteract these negative effects.

If you are breathing properly you will be using your diaphragm and not your ribs (intercostal muscles). Check this by lying on the floor or sitting upright in a chair with your feet flat on the floor and your back straight. Place your hands fingertip to fingertip over your belly button and breathe in slowly. Your fingers should come apart slightly.

Learning quick relaxation exercises to reduce tension in your body, and to let go of anxiety can be very helpful when you are quitting. Practise the exercises when you are relaxed before trying to use them when you are tense or anxious. There are 2 relaxation exercises and 2 meditations available via download. Listen to them freely as you read this book.

Mind and body links

There are extremely strong links between how we feel physically in our bodies, and how we think, process information and emotionally feel. So much so that an effective treatment for depression is the use of Botox to prevent us from being able to frown. If we frown we feel down. Conversely a bizarrely effective treatment for low mood is the half-smile, where you relax your face and turn your lips upwards. These 2 approaches work the same way: by affecting the signals muscles are sending to the brain. A frown sends 'we have a problem' signals, whereas the half-smile communicates 'all is well'.

We are more reactive and more negative when we are physically tense. Nicotine increases tension because it activates our Fight/Flight system. This means our heart rate rises, our blood pressure goes up, our breathing rate increases, and our muscles tense in readiness to fight off danger or run away quickly.

On the other hand, deep relaxation switches off that 'high alert' system, and instead activates our rest & recover system. Smokers and vapers spend far more time in a state of high alert than nonsmokers do. So it is very useful for them to learn ways of deeply relaxing muscles, which you can do using the downloaded relaxation scripts.

Relaxation Techniques

- **Body Scan Relaxation**

This takes you through your body allowing you to fully relax using cue words and visualisations, while releasing tension from all areas of the body.

- **Tension Release Breathing & Cue Controlled Relaxation**

This helps reduce stress by allowing you to deeply relax your muscles, and pairs a word with deep relaxation, so that if you practice the script regularly, then that word becomes a cue for deep relaxation. This means you will be able to let go of tension and relax anywhere, very quickly.

Meditations

There are 2 available via download and can be used at any time as you read the book and after quitting.

- **Mindfulness of Breathing Meditation**

This is a classic meditation, used to calm the mind and reconnect you to your own breath. With practice, the ability to reconnect to the breath anytime and anywhere becomes a powerful technique to help you avoid spiralling off into unhelpful thought cycles and heightened emotional states.

- **Embracing Life Meditation.**

This helps people to connect with peace and happiness through focusing on the gift of life, health, loved ones, nature and the endless positive possibilities available to us when we are open and present to them. This helps you enhance positive experiences, turn neutral experiences into more pleasurable ones, and calmly sit with negative feelings, rather than escaping to unhelpful coping strategies.

Products to help you

To help you overcome physical addiction to nicotine, there are several products available over the counter or on prescription. The main products available in the UK are Nicotine Replacement Therapies (NRT), Bupropion (Zyban) and Varenicline (Champix). NRT works by replacing some of the nicotine, which reduces the intensity of withdrawal symptoms and cravings. Bupropion and Varenicline, which are only available on prescription, do not contain any nicotine, but work directly on brain pathways that are affected by addictive processes.

Nicotine Replacement Therapy (NRT)

Smoking kills approximately half of all smokers due to the tar in cigarettes, and vapes have as yet unknown effects from the chemicals in the aerosols. It is not the nicotine in cigarettes or vapes that does the most damage – though that is harmful too.

NRT aims to replace the nicotine you get from smoking or vaping in different, safer ways. And – crucially – temporarily!

There are many ways of using NRT. The options available in the UK are:

- skin patches
- chewing gum
- under the tongue tablets
- lozenges
- nasal sprays
- inhalers

There are various brands available, and the products come in different strengths, but they all work in the same way: they provide an alternative method of getting nicotine.

All types of NRT are available on prescription to smokers over the age of eighteen. If you are under eighteen, your doctor may agree to prescribe them for you, but you will need to discuss this with them. If you have health problems or are pregnant or breast-feeding, then you can arrange to see your GP for a discussion about your health and medical history.

Smokers are already receiving nicotine when they smoke. Moreover, plasma nicotine levels from cigarettes are many times higher than those from NRT. This is because smoking a cigarette causes nicotine to be transported arterially via the carotid arteries, whereas NRT is transported in venous blood, and plasma levels are much lower.

In recognition of these factors, the guidelines from the National Institute for Health and Clinical Excellence (NICE, March 2002), recommend the use of NRT products in pregnancy, and with patients suffering serious illness. The NICE document reads: 'Smokers with certain conditions...are advised only to use NRT after careful consideration of risks and benefits and after discussion with a healthcare professional.' Similar advice applies to women who are pregnant or breast-feeding. When giving such advice to people in these groups who have been unable to quit smoking without using a cessation aid, health care professionals should take into account the significant harm associated with continuing to smoke and that it can be expected that NRT will deliver less nicotine and none of the other potentially disease-causing agents that would be obtained from cigarettes.'

Over a hundred trials have been conducted to look at the effectiveness of NRT and they clearly show that NRT can help people to stop smoking and vaping. [1]

In these trials one group of participants received NRT while another group was given a fake version or placebo. The results showed that people on NRT were almost twice as likely to quit smoking as those on the placebo. However, using NRT does not feel the same as smoking. NRT does not produce the same effects as a cigarette, and anyone who expects it to resemble smoking will be disappointed. NRT is not a cigarette substitute.

Key Concept

> NRT is extremely well researched. The evidence shows that it increases your chance of quitting success.

Ironically the most effective form of NRT is vaping. E-Cigarettes were meant to be used ONLY by adult smokers to help them quit tobacco. Of course, that is not what happened and vaping is now a huge health crisis in its own right.

The bizarre history of vaping is a master-class in the power of marketing, and of the importance of psychology in how easy or difficult things are to give up.

'Vapes' existed before vapes were invented – they were called inhalators or oral nicotine inhalers, and were just another form of NRT. They were sold in chemists with the other NRT products, and were of zero interest to anyone apart from the adult smokers trying to quit, who they were made for.

Then e-cigarettes came out in funky flavours, sold in head shops and heavily marketed to kids. The result is a global vape epidemic.

Research has even been done on why vapes are so popular when nicotine oral inhalers are not – with vapes being rated as offering more satisfaction, more social acceptability, more reward, and more 'coolness'. [3] I think we can all recognise that this translates to 'more well marketed and branded!'

The huge problem with vapes is that they are not used – even by adult smokers – as a smoking cessation aid but as a smoking *substitute*. Which might be a trade-off worth making if the alternative is life-long smoking. But comes with all the hassles and stress of life as a nicotine addict. Plus, the health risks of nicotine in any form become more relevant if you simply swap smoking for a different form of nicotine delivery system.

The fact that vaping is not viewed as a way to quit smoking, but as a 'cool', 'satisfying', 'rewarding', and 'socially acceptable' alternative to smoking means vaping is being taken up by children and young adults in their millions. A fact that has apparently passed the researchers by, as the study cited above concludes we should try and promote e-cigarettes:

"E-cigarettes have the potential to be important nicotine delivery products owing to their high acceptance and perceived benefit". [2]

A frankly astonishing conclusion on vaping that comes from a respected medical journal, not, as you might imagine, from a vape manufacturer!

Official Advice comes with a Health Warning

Official health advice around smoking and vaping has always been naive, muddle-headed and obtuse. (Or possibly wilfully, cynically wrong due to vested interests. Take your pick). From the decades it took for successive governments to even admit tobacco was harmful, to the oft repeated reassurance that vaping would never be of interest to non-smokers.

I have the same feeling today reading the following quote from Better Health, an NHS site, as I had years ago when I heard those idiotic suits promoting vaping as the solution to smoking, confidently asserting that vapes would never be used by anyone else, despite multiple loud warnings that this was naive nonsense.

Better Health writes:

"Nicotine vaping is substantially less harmful than smoking. It's also one of the most effective tools for quitting smoking."

That advice is based on the simplistic assumption that 1 puff of a vape is less harmful than 1 puff of a cigarette.

Just like the previously held view that 'there is no evidence any non-smoker will ever use vapes', the current advice ignores human behaviour, is utterly ignorant of trends, and glosses over the unknowns.

One puff of a vape may well be less harmful than one puff of a cigarette. Though, in reality, one puff of either won't do anyone any harm. The problem isn't the 1 puff, it's the millions of puffs: i.e. the long-term behaviours of smokers and vapers. And the reality is that most smokers who try to quit by vaping end up using **both**. AND most smokers who do fully switch to vaping, end up going back to smoking – very often at higher levels than before.

Dual Use

Dual use is a major issue with smokers who switch to vaping, with studies showing that the vast majority of former smokers who vape now use both. The health impact of dual use is **worse** than that of smoking cigarettes alone. [4] A comprehensive review of over 100 studies showed a 20-40% increase in risk of heart disease, asthma, COPD, metabolic disorders and oral diseases with dual use. [3]

Dual use also allows for a very large intake of nicotine.

Vapers returning to smoking.

Most smokers who switch to vaping, end up going back to smoking, and many smoke far MORE after their brief dalliance with vapes, because of how much more nicotine you can get from vapes than from cigarettes. This is because:

a)   Vapes don't make you throw up the way excessive tobacco can, which means vapers can tolerate far higher consumption levels at far younger ages.

b)   Vaping is done anywhere and everywhere: bedrooms, in the pub, in the kitchen, airport toilets, on trains. I know someone who was in hospital for a surgery and stayed there for a few nights. Every hour she would get up and vape in the hospital bathroom. Smokers also smoke while in hospital, but not until they are ambulatory enough to drag their drip stands outside.

c) Vaping does not involve regular natural stopping points, which occur after each cigarette.

It is no surprise that people tend to smoke in multiples of 10 or 20. A twenty a day smoker will be reluctant to start a 2nd pack, so they stay on 20 a day for ages, until eventually this is no longer enough. However, once that 2nd pack is open, the 20 a day becomes 40 a day quite quickly. But there is no immediate feedback with vapes that alerts you to how much you are vaping, and so vapers are not encouraged or forced into a degree of moderation. A 600 puff elf bar is the equivalent of at least 20 cigarettes (which is the NHS figure and therefore to be taken with a sackful of salt. Some doctors believe it's actually the equivalent of 40-50 cigarettes). That's 600 uninterrupted puffs, with no feedback as to what you've puffed your way through.

It is very common for a 20 a day smoker to try and quit with vaping, use both for a while, and then go back to smoking and discover they now need 40 a day. This is not helpful! It is also increasingly common for vapers to try smoking to help them quit vaping, in a stunningly ironic twist.

Finally, the dangers of vaping are becoming clearer and clearer all the time and will, I am sure, be laid bare in the decades ahead.

I firmly believe that all that advice will have to be changed or ditched when the true extent of the harm caused by vaping becomes clear. At which time the unnecessary damage inflicted on an entire generation will become painfully and shockingly obvious. Along with the unintended consequences of the current advice, such as dual use and returning to higher levels of smoking than ever before.

So please be very careful before taking false comfort from advice to vape instead of smoke.

I support the use of NRT as a temporary measure while you tackle the overall Nicotine Addiction Triangle. I do **not** support the use of vaping as a life-long alternative to smoking, which will just keep you trapped in a different addiction prison, and which has all sorts of other risks associated with it.

But NRT is nicotine, and nicotine is the problem, so how can it help?

While people can and do get hooked on NRT, they do so at far lower rates than those people now hooked on e-cigarettes. This even includes the inhalator, which basically is a vape. But a boringly unsexy version of one.

On the other hand, there is a growing problem with the use of Snus among young people - powdered tobacco you place between lips and gums. This has always been popular in Sweden, but is increasingly common in the UK among young people who have never smoked or vaped.

Snus is, of course, highly addictive, and in common with other forms of tobacco, can cause cancer, especially oral and oesophageal cancers, and also pancreatic cancer.

In theory, there is nothing much different about NRT lozenges and Snus, or between the inhalator and a vape, but in this game it is ALL about the marketing.

The relative lack of dependency to NRT is simply because the vape-peddlers, Snus lovers, (and their enablers in government and health settings who call them safe), are selling the psychology of the dependency, along with the nicotine. As NRT is only available in boring places, it rarely becomes a trend. Or not yet anyway.

A clear caveat is that NRT should ONLY be used by someone

trying to quit a different type of nicotine dependency, only ever used TEMPORARILY, and ALWAYS with the aim of becoming completely nicotine free. If you use NRT like that, then you do so knowing you are just getting some help with angle 1 of the Nicotine Addiction Triangle - while you work on angles 2 & 3.

On the other hand, if you go to a head shop to try this cool new thing called Snus, that everyone on your corridor at university is raving about, you are already suckered by angle 2, and are creating brand new problems with angles 1 and 3. So you will get completely stuck in all 3 angles very quickly.

Ironically, the fact that boring old NRT, taken in any form, 'works' with little dependency, while well marketed new forms of nicotine hook people really fast, just shows you how pointless ALL nicotine use is. And how strong the psychological element is. But if you are already hooked, NRT can take the edge off one part of the problem while you deal with the other aspects.

Which NRT product you choose is a matter of personal preference. They all work in the same way in that they replace the nicotine you currently get from cigarettes, which reduces physical withdrawal symptoms and cravings. Studies show that they all work equally well.

It is important that you choose the correct strength, and your doctor or pharmacist can help you with that. Do not try to make do with less than you need. It will not make corning off the NRT any easier and may mean you fail to stop smoking. Studies suggest that using as much as you need is important in giving you the best chance of success.

Side effects are rare and not serious. Some people are sensitive to the glue on the patches. Others experience irritation of the nose and eyes with the nasal sprays. Feel free to experiment with different types of NRT to see which one suits you. Some people suffer minor sleep disturbances, though this may also be caused by stopping smoking.

The products

Transdermal (skin) patches are worn for either sixteen or twenty-four hours per day. They are available in 5, 10 and 15 mg strengths, or 7, 14 and 21 mg strengths, depending on the brand. Some health professionals advise you to reduce the strength of the patch as your quit attempt continues (e.g. take each strength for four weeks, for a total course of twelve weeks). If you wish to do this that is fine. The logic behind this is to make it easier to come off the patch. However, there is very little evidence that people find coming off the patch hard (though this is not true of other types of NRT).

On the other hand, there is evidence that using reduced doses of NRT makes quitting less likely. If you feel confident that you can reduce the dose, then do so, as it can be powerfully motivating and make you feel that you are making progress. But if you are struggling, stay on the higher dose.

Similarly, if at the end of the course you feel you are coping fine and can come off the drug, then do so and congratulations! But if you are still struggling, take NRT for longer.

Chewing gum is available in 2 or 4 mg strengths and can be chewed for several hours at a time. Some people find the taste awful at first, but then they did not like the taste of cigarettes either. It is possible to get hooked on gum. Some people have been on it for years, and find it just as hard to give up as cigarettes. To avoid this, try to stick to the eight- or twelve-week programme.

Under-the-tongue tablets and lozenges are (obviously!) placed under the tongue and allowed to dissolve. Tablets come in 2mg strength while lozenges are available in 1, 2 and 4 mg.

Nasal sprays deliver 0.5mg of nicotine per spray. These take a little while to get the hang of, and some people hate the sensation at first.

Nasal sprays and inhalers deliver nicotine quite quickly, so some people prefer them to the products that are taken by mouth or through the skin.

Inhalers are cigarette-shaped holders with a cartridge that contains 10mg of nicotine. You inhale the nicotine by sucking on the holder in the same way as with a cigarette. This does not mean the inhalers feel like smoking cigarettes. The aim of NRT is to replace some of the nicotine, not to replace smoking.

Vapes are e-cigarettes that do make stopping smoking tobacco easier, but the way they have been marketed means they are themselves now a major problem, and are usually used as a substitute to smoking, not as a way of quitting nicotine altogether.

> ## Key Concept
>
> All forms and brands of NRT work in the same way and all are equally effective. Choose whichever you prefer.

Long-term use

Nicotine in any form is an addictive drug. You can therefore get hooked on NRT. Nicotine has been compulsively used in many different forms across cultures and throughout history. There is nothing special about a cigarette. Cigarettes just happen to be the way we get nicotine. If we lived in a different time or place we might instead be tobacco chewers or snuff users. Some Asian communities use paan, a paste containing nicotine which is rubbed on the gums.

If you get hooked on NRT, or you switch to vaping from smoking, you will at least be spared the 4,000 toxic chemicals that make cigarettes so deadly. But you will still be a nicotine addict and will still suffer the hassle and expense of living with Nitch. You will keep experiencing withdrawal symptoms and will have all the psychological dependency problems that make life as a smoker so unpleasant. You will not be free. If you ever go somewhere where your product is not available you will either need to fill your suitcases with NRT or go back to smoking. My hopes for you therefore are not merely that you switch from cigarettes to NRT but that you become free of the addiction altogether. If being an NRT addict seems attractive to you, re-read the first few chapters, switching the word NRT for cigarette. Life as a smoker is difficult and stressful quite apart from the health consequences. Life as an NRT addict is just as difficult for the same reasons.

Key Concept

Nicotine is addictive in any form - including NRT.

If you feel at risk of developing an NRT dependence, or if you have been hooked on NRT in the past, then try patches, as these have the least potential for longer-term addiction. This is not because the patch is not addictive - it is. However, addiction is much more powerful when psychological dependence begins to develop.

With any form of nicotine use, you get physically hooked first. Then beliefs and attitudes about the importance of the drug begin to develop, and psychological dependence is created, as we have seen with cigarettes and vapes.

If you use chewing gum, beliefs also often develop about how great the chewing action feels and how good it tastes. With most forms of NRT you actually have to do something, such as inhale, spray or chew. With under-the-tongue NRT you experience the taste. Patches are the only form of NRT where, apart from slapping the thing on, you do nothing and feel nothing. For this reason, it is harder to develop positive beliefs about the product, and therefore makes it harder to develop psychological dependence.

However, these beliefs take time to develop, so you can safely use all the products for at least the eight to twelve weeks suggested. Just keep in mind that switching permanently to NRT is not the aim, and make sure that if you start 'liking' the NRT a bit too much, you come off it or switch to a patch.

Key Concept

There is little risk of getting hooked on patches. This is not true of all other types of NRT.

There are some advantages to using types of NRT that require conscious effort, because many people find it helpful actually to do something to help them get through a particularly difficult situation, such as a party. Slipping a lozenge under the tongue, for example, can provide the confidence needed to stay off cigarettes in high-risk circumstances.

Using more than one type

NRT products are licensed to be used singly. In other words, only one product at a time. You will therefore probably be prescribed only one type of NRT. However, there are studies that show that using two types at a time is more effective than just one. Some people, for example, like to have a patch on all the time to give them a base-line of nicotine, but also to use a different form of NRT several times throughout the day when they feel they need a bit of a boost.

There is very little risk of overdosing on nicotine using NRT. People have access to large amounts of nicotine in their cigarette packets and vapes. They manage, without advice from their pharmacists or GPs, to inhale as much nicotine as they need from each cigarette. People can smoke strong or weak cigarettes, and even if they have no idea whether a cigarette is high, medium or low in nicotine, they can still regulate the dose so that they get as much nicotine as they want. People will cadge strong roll-ups and smoke them without overdosing, even if normally they smoke ultra-mild cigarettes. So don't worry about using too much NRT.

Dual use is a major issue, however, with smokers who switch to vaping. Studies show that the vast majority of former smokers who vape now use both. Dual use also allows for a very large intake of nicotine, which often means smoking more than ever if you switch back. Which many people do.

Despite the advice that vaping is the best way to quit, my strong advice is absolutely not to try vaping to quit smoking. Vapes are considerably less harmful than tobacco-based cigarettes, so switch from smoking to vapes if you honestly don't think you can quit completely, in order to reduce smoking related harm. But this must be a total and permanent switch from one form of nicotine for another. Unless you switch completely and permanently, you are likely to end up worse off than before, either using both, or going back to smoking, but potentially smoking more than before.

How it works (and why it might not...)

NRT works by replacing some of the nicotine you currently get from smoking or vaping. This should in turn lessen cravings and make quitting easier. But remember, cravings are only partly physical. NRT does not stop you wanting or missing your habit if your internal script is telling you cigarettes and e-cigs are special. NRT does not stop psychological dependence. If you are in the right frame of mind for quitting, NRT can be very helpful in reducing physical withdrawal symptoms. If you are in the wrong frame of mind, it will not work for you.

Key Concept
NRT can help you overcome physical addiction, (angle 1), but it does not address psychological dependence.

Bupropion (Zyban)

Bupropion is a prescription-only drug, made by GlaxoSmithKline, and marketed under the brand name Zyban. Bupropion is not considered suitable if you are pregnant or breast-feeding, or if you are under eighteen.

Some GPs will prescribe bupropion only if you are also willing to receive counselling and/or motivational support. This is a good idea as your chances of success are considerably higher if you have professional support along the way.

There are free smoking-cessation services available worldwide. Many of these will not specifically address psychological dependence as very few services are psychology-led or have input from clinical psychology. However, they can provide support, encouragement, advice on product use and health information.

Key Concept

Bupropion is available only on prescription. Talk to your GP or local smoking cessation service if you want to try it.

Bupropion works on brain pathways that are involved in addiction and withdrawal, but exactly how it works is not clear. It is nicotine-free and non-addictive, and trials have shown that it is successful in helping people stop smoking. It appears that Zyban's effects are similar to NRT in that it roughly doubles your quit rate.

Key Concept

Unlike NRT, Bupropion is not addictive.

Smokers using Bupropion describe their cigarettes as tasting awful or failing to satisfy them anymore. It is rather like smoking nicotine-free or ultra-low-yield cigarettes - they taste and smell like cigarettes, but they just do not do the job. If cigarettes are less satisfying it then becomes easier to give them up, and many people feel that as long as they are still on the bupropion there is no point in smoking. Smokers also experience fewer withdrawal symptoms and fewer cravings. It is likely that the same will be true for vapers.

Side effects

Certain side effects are associated with bupropion and it is important that you discuss the risks with your doctor before starting treatment. The most clinically important is an increased risk of seizures. These occur in 0.1% of cases, i.e. one in a thousand patients. For this reason, Bupropion will not be prescribed for you if you have a history of seizures, or if you have any of the other risk factors for a lowered seizure threshold. These risk factors include:

- prior seizure

- history of head injury

- central nervous system tumour

- taking other medications known to lower seizure threshold, including some antidepressants, antipsychotics, theophylline, systemic steroids, quinolone antibiotics and antimalarials

- excessive use of alcohol

- rapid withdrawal from alcohol or tranquillisers

- diabetes treated with hypoglycaemics or insulin

- use of over-the-counter stimulants

- addiction to opiates, cocaine or stimulants

- history of anorexia or bulimia nervosa (serious eating disorders)

If you are taking another medication that reduces the seizure threshold, but would like to try bupropion, it may be possible for your GP to switch you to a different medication so that it is safe for you to have both. At least fourteen days should elapse between discontinuation of one drug and the start of the other. If you have a seizure while taking bupropion, you must stop the medication and inform your GP.

Other possible side effects include allergic reactions, which in rare cases can be severe. If you have a severe allergic reaction soon after starting bupropion you must stop taking it, even though it is often difficult to pin down exactly what it is you are sensitive to. Some people may suffer a milder allergic reaction. In this case, discuss your concerns with your doctor. It may be wise to stop the drug and see if the symptoms disappear.

More common side effects include insomnia, dry mouth, agitation, depression or stomach upsets. These are not serious and usually settle down within a week or two. If you experience some side effects but also notice clear benefits you need to decide how much discomfort you are willing to put up with in order to quit smoking. It is worth bearing in mind that many of the side effects are also symptoms of nicotine withdrawal so your discomfort might not even be due to the bupropion.

Using Bupropion

The course of bupropion is eight weeks long. One tablet a day should be taken for the first six days, then two tablets a day for the rest of the course. If you experience uncomfortable side effects then continue with one tablet a day. The drug takes a few days to reach maximum levels in your bloodstream, so you should wait until the second week of taking the drug before you stop smoking or vaping. Some people find that their cigarettes and e-cigs are less and less satisfying as the days go by, and that by their quit date they are quite happy to give up. Other people do not notice any difference in their experience of vaping or smoking, but have fewer withdrawal symptoms and cravings when they stop. At the end of the eight-week course, you should have been a non-smoker for about six weeks. By this time most nicotine withdrawal is complete, and coming off the bupropion should not be a problem. If you suddenly experience intense cravings again, then these are probably due to psychological factors, and we shall deal with them in the next chapter.

People who use bupropion for several weeks often find that towards the end of the course they forget to take their tablets for several days and do not even notice the difference. This makes sense because by this stage of quitting you will have very little, if any, nicotine left in your system.

However, some people view the tablets as having mythical and magical properties and expect to be swamped with cravings as soon as the course ends. And, surprise surprise, this is exactly what happens. The problem is not the bupropion, or the nicotine. It is the mind. NRT and bupropion can really help you get off nicotine. But staying free involves more than simply getting rid of the physical dependence. You need to get rid of the psychological dependence too. The importance of this was neatly captured by a member of one of my groups. 'That Zyban is bloomin' awful,' he said. 'It makes my cigarettes taste terrible. I had to stop taking it so I could enjoy a fag again!'

Varenicline (Chantix)

Varenicline is another drug that works by reducing cravings for nicotine and blocking its effect on the brain, while also helping with withdrawal symptoms such as feeling irritable or having difficulty sleeping. Varenicline was withdrawn from sale in the UK and Europe in 2022, but became available once again in 2024.

Evidence suggests it's the most effective medicine for helping people to stop smoking, with one study directly comparing it with Bupropion and finding better outcomes.

Who can take it

Most people can take varenicline, although there are some situations where it's not recommended. For example, it's not suitable:

- for children under 18 years old
- if you're pregnant or breastfeeding
- if you have severe kidney problems

Possible side effects

Side effects of varenicline can include:

- feeling and being sick
- difficulty sleeping (insomnia), sometimes with vivid dreams
- dry mouth
- constipation or diarrhoea
- headaches
- feeling drowsy
- feeling dizzy

Like any other treatment, it only deals with 1 angle – it does not address psychological dependence.

Chapter Summary

- Angle 1 is nicotine addiction.

- NRT increases your chance of success.

- NRT is in itself addictive, so take care to use it purely to help you overcome physical dependence, and beware the risk of developing psychological dependence if you use it for too long.

- Patches are the least likely to cause this problem.

- Bupropion (Zyban) and Varenicline (Chantix) are medications that can also help.

- The relaxation and meditation downloads available from the website can help address the tension stemming from withdrawal, and increase resilience so you can cope better with the difficult first few days.

Chapter 11: Overcoming Psychological Dependence & Habit

By now you should be feeling that life free from all forms of nicotine is something positive rather than something negative. Many people enter a quit attempt feeling utterly miserable at the thought of everything they are giving up. The beliefs, developed over years, make them think of their cigarettes or vapes as something helpful, pleasurable or necessary.

These beliefs are untrue. Giving up nicotine is nothing more than giving up the need to keep using nicotine.

The need to feed Nitch is a time-consuming and expensive nuisance at best, and at worst leaves you climbing the walls with desperation. It ranges from the slightly on-edge feeling you get when you are at a dinner party and no one else has had a puff or nipped outside, to the restless anxiety of someone who has run out on the motorway and is late for a meeting, but needs to stop anyway to buy some more, to the frantic need that drives you out at 3 a.m. in a blizzard to get relief, to the utter desperation that leads you to smoke through a hole in your neck on the fire escape of the hospital ward, 15 hours after surgery.

The only reason to smoke or vape is because you need to. All that the nicotine hit achieves is to stop you needing to - for an hour or so. **This need never dies.** It continues getting stronger and stronger and stronger until you die - or quit. You will never quit without making a deliberate and conscious effort to do so. Do not waste your time hoping that one day you will just not want to anymore. The fact is, you already do not want to, but you are an addict so you have to, no matter how inconvenient or horrible. And that will never change until you stop being an addict.

Ask yourself 2 questions:

- Am I happy to do this for life? If the answer is no, the 2nd question becomes:

- Well if not now, then when?

I finally gave up smoking after many, many failed attempts. Even though I had quit on many previous occasions, that final time really was different. In all my earlier quit attempts I assumed that smoking was a pleasure and made me feel good, but that it was unhealthy and so I needed to quit. Smoking scared me, but I also felt as if I could not manage without it. Every few months I would make another quit attempt, and sometimes these would last a few weeks.

When I got through the first few weeks I tended to find that I was coping okay without smoking - most of the time - but there would still always be situations when I suddenly felt as if I was missing out, and I had cravings again. Inevitably I would tell myself that the odd smoke now and again did no harm, and I would get hooked again. It would then take me months to psych myself up for another attempt.

When I eventually quit properly, I saw smoking for what it really was. At home alone, I took a cigarette out of the packet and was just about to light up when I had that moment of clarity I described earlier. It was so powerful and compelling that suddenly I could see what a miserable existence smokers have. There was nothing good about smoking, it just stopped you feeling bad. But the only reason you feel bad is because you smoke. The only solution - quit and be free of the bully you've spent years pandering to.

People only smoke to feel like non-smokers!

Key Concept

Smokers don't understand the drive to smoke, so they develop positive beliefs about smoking that provide an explanation.

Some people experience a similar eye-opening flash and quit abruptly with no problem. In my groups these people leave the session saying, 'that's it, never again,' and stop smoking there and then. However, for most people it is not as simple or quick as that, so do not panic if you still feel worried about quitting. Most people gradually come to realise how nicotine addiction really works, and the longer they abstain, the more clearly they can see this reality. Nothing clouds your thinking like addiction, so until you are physically free, you are likely to find it hard to grasp fully how great you will feel to be shot of the whole business. But you will feel great, and you will feel free.

Use the worksheets at the end of the chapter to help you overcome Nitch's propaganda.

When you first stop there will be certain situations that are particularly difficult. This is because you will have been conditioned to see smoking as pleasurable or helpful in those situations.

Conditioning is a well-understood process. To overcome habitual nicotine use, you need to break all your associations between nicotine and other parts of your life and allow the conditioning to fade away. The tips discussed in Chapter 8 can speed up this process.

You may also find it helpful to learn some coping strategies to deal with the temporary difficulties involved in killing Nitch. These include distraction, relaxation techniques, meditation and hypnosis.

Distraction

If you have a craving and need something to take your mind off it, try any or all of the following:

- Count backwards from 100 in 7s (100, 93, 86 and so on).

- Think of capital cities beginning with A,B,C right through to Z.

- Wear a rubber band around your wrist and flick it. (Sounds weird but it does sometimes help!)

- Play a favourite song.

- Play a computer game.

- Go for a walk.

Relaxation Techniques

As noted before, learning deep relaxation skills will be very helpful to all smokers, to counteract these negative thoughts and feelings. Meditations can also dramatically boost wellbeing.

A few years ago, I was working in an adult mental health department. The department waiting list included many people who had serious problems with anxiety. While they were waiting for individual treatment, I taught them all either a relaxation exercise, or a type of meditation called Mindfulness of Breathing. I then compared their effectiveness.

I was testing out the idea that meditation would be better at relieving anxiety than straightforward relaxation, because meditation includes your mind, not just your body. In meditation you physically relax your body while at the same time learning to quieten your mind. This is very helpful in anxiety, since anxiety generally involves fretting and worrying about things in the future. Learning to stay focused on the here and now is an extremely useful skill.

Another helpful aspect of meditation is that it helps people learn to accept negative emotions calmly, and then gently to let those emotions go. In meditation you are aware of exactly how you are feeling, and you simply let yourself feel those emotions, without trying to push them away. Then slowly re-focus on your breathing and the negativity drifts away. My research showed that both relaxation and meditation work well to help people cope better with anxiety, but that meditation was more effective.

More recently there has been a lot of additional research into meditation which has shown that it reduces the risk of developing depression and anxiety in people who have had these sorts of problems in the past. This meditation is a fundamental part of Buddhist practice but when used in the context of the NHS, it is separate from any spiritual or religious dimension. You do not need to have any religious beliefs or interests in order to benefit from mindfulness meditation.

Use the downloads to practice the 2 meditations.

• **Mindfulness of Breathing Meditation**

This is a classic meditation, used to calm the mind and reconnect you to your own breath. With practice, the ability to reconnect to the breath anytime and anywhere becomes a powerful technique to help you avoid spiralling off into unhelpful thought cycles and heightened emotional states.

- **Embracing Life Meditation**

This helps people to connect with peace and happiness through focusing on the gift of life, loved ones, nature and the endless positive possibilities available to us when we are open and present to them. This also helps you learn to sit with more difficult feelings, and manage them more thoughtfully and skilfully, rather than escaping to unhelpful coping strategies.

Self-Hypnosis

Hypnosis has been described as "the playful imagining of positive possibilities".

Hypnosis is a structured approach using natural psychological processes to achieve positive therapeutic change or to achieve specific goals. Hypnosis chiefly uses fixed attention on a single idea or set of ideas, along with our natural suggestibility, and the ability to strengthen or weaken thoughts, beliefs and emotional states. These processes are active in us all day long – but we generally have little control over them. We get ideas fixed in our mind like 'I can't quit', or 'I need a smoke to relax'. Or we experience emotions like dread or overwhelm. We accept these thoughts and feelings as if they are true reflections on us or our lives, and often act on them. Our minds run our lives and get in the way of our goals, instead of the other way around.

Hypnosis puts us – the human - back in control, and helps the mind to work for us and not against us.

The hypnosis downloads guide you into a deep state of relaxation (sometimes described as a trance-like state) and while you're in this state you are more receptive to vivid imagining of positive possibilities in your life, more able to make use of suggestions, and to overcome fears, increase confidence, and achieve goals.

How does hypnosis work?

Hypnosis combines psychological, motivational, attentional and relaxation approaches to dramatically boost self-belief, confidence, focus, and present moment awareness. Hypnosis turbo charges the changes in thoughts and feelings that this book is encouraging, by embedding them more deeply, and increasing a person's trust in themselves, their abilities to cope without nicotine, and in the strategies they are using.

Hypnosis declutters the mind and that means you are in a heightened state of focus and clarity. This makes you more open to suggestions or advice, and you process ideas more deeply, and accept them more fully. The ideas can then take root, and lead to meaningful and rapid changes in how you think, feel and behave in your real life. You will remain awake and aware throughout and are always in control.

Brain imaging studies show that the brain responds in unique ways to being hypnotised. The effects of hypnosis are real and can be scientifically explained.

There are 4 self-hypnosis scripts available via download. Each one of these can help with different parts of the problem.

The scripts are described below, along with guidance on when during the process you should listen to them for maximum impact.

- **Motivation and Commitment script**

This enhances your commitment to quitting and your desire for a life free of smoking, while giving you confidence and resilience that you can succeed. You need understand the Nicotine Addiction Triangle for this script to make sense.

- **Two Futures script**

This sets out 2 future paths and cements your choice of the path to freedom. Use this after you have read and understood the Nicotine Addiction Triangle fully and are making the firm decision to quit. You should play this script on quit date and then throw all your smoking materials away as soon as you have listened to it. Then repeat whenever you feel you are wavering.

- Thought Stopping

- Relapse Prevention

The final 2 scripts are to be used after you have quit to deal with urges and cravings to smoke again. They are described more fully in the Relapse Prevention chapter (chapter 13).

Chapter summary

- Overcoming Nitch's propaganda can take time and patience.

- Overcoming habits can also take time, so don't panic if things feel difficult at first.

- Learning relaxation and meditation techniques can be very helpful.

- Self-hypnosis is a powerful tool to enhance the messages in this book and embed them firmly in your mind.

- The downloads provided cover relaxation, meditation and smoking specific self-hypnosis for motivation and commitment.

Listed below are a number of different situations that commonly cause people anxiety when they quit. The worksheet takes you through the links between the situation itself, the thoughts that can arise in those situations, and the feelings the quitter then has. Note the feelings are not caused by the **situation** but by the

thoughts about the situation. There is a huge difference!

Situation

A) Sitting in a pub beer garden seeing a smoker light up with a satisfied sigh.

B) Waking up on quit date.

C) The first evening of a holiday.

D) At work struggling with something.

E) At home in the evening with the 'I want a cigarette/ e-cig' feeling.

Conditioned Thoughts

A) Lucky git, he gets to smoke. I bet he's really relaxed. I can't relax without a smoke. It's not fair.

B) How will I survive today? It's going to be terrible.

C) I can't believe I'm not smoking/vaping. It will ruin the holiday.

D) I can't concentrate. I'll never get this done without a puff.

E) I can't cope with this.

Feelings

A) Miserable, jealous, deprived, frustrated

B) Anxious, dreading it

C) Feeling of missing out, loss and deprivation

D) Frustrated and distracted

E) Restless, unsettled

Now have a look at each situation again, but with more rational and constructive thoughts. Note how this then changes the feelings.

Situation A:

Sitting in a pub beer garden, seeing a smoker light up with a satisfied sigh.

Rational Thoughts

He has no choice but to smoke. He will also be smoking tomorrow morning, the next day and the day after that. Look at him squinting away from the smoke. It looks uncomfortable. I don't have to do that anymore. I can focus on the good things here: Sunshine, cold beer/wine, friends. I'm going to have a great time.

Feelings

Relief to be free of it. Pleased with myself.

Situation B:

Waking in the morning on quit date.

Rational Thoughts

Don't panic. I never smoked till lunchtime anyway. Withdrawal symptoms aren't that bad - remember the week I spent in hospital? I will be fine. And if I don't like withdrawal, I need to remember that it is nicotine that CAUSES withdrawal. I never want to feel like this again, and the only way I can achieve that is by not smoking again.

Feelings

Calmer, more motivated.

Situation C:

The first evening of a holiday.

Rational Thoughts

I can enjoy everything good about this - the sun, the company, the break from work, the delicious food & drink. I am missing a false memory and absolutely nothing else. Nitch used to RUIN holidays, getting in the way all the time, making me leave my friends and stand outside.

Feelings

Happy and looking forward to the holiday.

Situation D:

At work struggling with something.

Rational Thoughts

Nitch is distracting me. If I feed him today, he will distract me tomorrow, and forever. This distraction will pass soon. Just take a deep breath, and re-focus.

Feelings

More positive & focused.

Situation E:

At home in the evening with the 'I want a cigarette/vape' feeling.

Rational Thoughts

Nitch is winding me up. I am killing him off (hurrah) and he doesn't like it. GOOD!

Cigarettes cause these horrible feelings. If I ignore them or just accept them soon Nitch will be dead, and I will be free.

Feelings

Determined, motivated.

Worksheet

The aim of this worksheet is to teach you the importance of your thoughts. Thoughts strongly affect feelings. To feel positive and confident, you need to think positively and confidently.

Worksheet

The next step is for you to identify your own negative thoughts. You need to recognise the little 'Nitchisms' that creep into your mind, making you feel anxious or miserable. Then you need to know how to replace the Nitchisms with more positive and realistic thoughts, that will help you think and feel differently about not smoking.

Worksheet

1) Think of situations you expect to find difficult.

2) Write down the sorts of things Nitch might say to you.

3) Anticipate how that might make you feel.

4) Develop more positive and rational thoughts about the situations.

5) Recognise the different feelings that this will lead to.

6) Arm yourself with some positive statements that you can use when you are in those situations.

Worksheet

The Motivation & Commitment self-hypnosis download can be used to deeply embed new ways of thinking and new ways of feeling into your mind. Do this exercise carefully then write out a list of positive statements so that you can rapidly access these in challenging situations.

Develop a positive affirmation that makes you feel excited and positive about life free from Nitch. During the self-hypnosis script you will be invited to silently repeat your affirmation to yourself, so make sure you have one ready before you listen.

Play the recording regularly.

....

....

....

....

....

....

....

....

....

....

....

....

....

Chapter 12:
Benefits of Quitting

By now I hope you will feel that there are no good reasons to carry on using nicotine in any form. So now we can turn to the other side of the coin - all the excellent reasons for quitting. The following facts about smoking are frightening. Smokers do not like to think about the facts of smoking because, naturally, they become anxious and scared by the appalling costs. If you are about to quit, then knowing these facts can help spur you on. If you feel that the facts will just panic you then skip the next section and read 'Health benefits of quitting' instead. Later on in your quit attempt, come back to this section to discover all the dreadful things that are now much less likely to happen to you.

Health risks of smoking

- Smoking is the single biggest preventable cause of death and illness in the UK.

- Half of all lifelong smokers will die from their smoking.

- After the age of 40, every year you smoke knocks 3 months off your life - a quarter of every year.

- Smoking is responsible for 84% of deaths from lung cancer.

- Smoking is responsible for 83% of deaths from lung diseases such as bronchitis and emphysema.

- Smokers have more than twice as much chance of having a heart attack as non-smokers.

- Smoking causes cancers of the lung, mouth, larynx,

breast, oesophagus, bladder, kidney, stomach, cervix and pancreas.

- Tobacco harms almost every living tissue in the body that it comes in contact with.

- Smoking is linked to asthma and brittle bone disease.

- Smoking in pregnancy increases your risk of miscarriage by 27%. It also increases your risk of infant illness and low birth weight.

- Smoking is the main contributor to cot death.

- Smoking increases risks of impotence and infertility.

- Smoking doubles your risk of going blind.

Health Risks of Vaping

Vaping turns liquid into a mist that people breathe in, coating the lungs with chemicals. Some of the vaporized elements of the oil get deep down into the lungs causing an inflammatory response. E-liquid usually includes flavorings, aromatic additives and nicotine or THC (the chemical in marijuana that causes psychological effects), dissolved in an oily liquid base, often thickened with Vitamin E. This is safe when taken orally as a supplement or used on the skin, but is an irritant when inhaled. It's been found in the lungs of people with severe, vaping-related damage.

Other common substances found in e-liquid or produced when it's heated up which also pose a risk to the lungs include:

Diacetyl: This food additive, used to deepen e-cigarette flavours, is known to damage small passageways in the lungs. Many vapes use diacetyl, though it is banned in the UK.

Formaldehyde: This toxic chemical can cause lung disease and contribute to heart disease.

Acrolein: Most often used as a weed killer.

Several lung diseases are associated with vaping:

Popcorn Lung

"Popcorn lung" is another name for bronchiolitis obliterans (BO), a rare condition that results from damage of the lungs' small airways caused by diacetyl. Diacetyl is frequently added to flavored e-liquid to enhance the taste in many countries, though not the UK. Inhaling diacetyl causes inflammation and may lead to permanent scarring in the smallest branches of the airways — popcorn lung — which makes breathing difficult. Popcorn lung has no lasting treatment.

Lipoid Pneumonia

Lipoid pneumonia develops when fatty acids enter the lungs. Vaping-related lipoid pneumonia is the result of inhaling oily substances found in e-liquid, which sparks an inflammatory response in the lungs.

Collapsed Lung

Collapsed lung occurs when air blisters on the top of the lungs rupture and create tiny tears. Smoking and vaping are associated with an increased risk of bursting these blisters, leading to lung collapse. This often happens to younger people and can lead to the need for surgery, or even be life threatening.

It is wonderful that you can avoid these horrendous risks by quitting, but the news is even better than that. You do not have to wait decades to benefit from quitting. You can benefit immediately.

Health Benefits of Quitting

Day 1:

Within 20 minutes heart rate and blood pressure starts to return back to normal.

Within 8 hours carbon monoxide starts to leave the body.

Within 24 hours excess mucus and debris are beginning to clear out of your lungs.

After 48 hours nicotine has all gone.

Within 72 hours your breathing becomes easier and your airways clearer. You have more energy.

Within 2-12 weeks:

Your circulation improves and you feel fitter.

Heart health is improving.

Within 3-9 months:

Your lung function increases by up to 10%.

You have fewer coughs and less wheezing.

Within 1 year:

You have halved your risk of heart disease.

Within 2 years:

Your risk of a heart attack is now the same as for a lifelong non-smoker.

Within 5-15 years:

Your risk of stroke is now the same as for lifelong non-smoker.

Within 10 years:

You have achieved a 50% reduction in the risk of lung cancer.

Chapter 13:
Relapse Prevention

Before you actually quit, you need to be absolutely clear that you will never smoke again. Ever! Before quitting it is useful to be aware of pitfalls so you can avoid falling back into the Nicotine Addiction Trap. Forewarned is forearmed.

Avoiding the Pitfalls

When you first quit you will be thinking about cigarettes or e-cigs a lot of the time. Thoughts, cravings and pangs of anxiety will occur frequently. Remember that this is temporary. Remind yourself that the desire for nicotine is a chemically induced state of anxiety, plus a load of propaganda, which will stay with you forever if you keep feeding Nitch, and will disappear forever when you quit.

> ## Key Concept
>
> The withdrawal symptoms you struggle with when you are trying to quit will stay with you forever if you carry on, but will disappear forever when you quit.

Visualise the danger signal slowly winding down till it sputters out for good. Now visualise resetting the danger signal by taking in nicotine. Recognise that this just means re-creating the problem. So if you reset the faulty signal you would have to go through the whole process all over again next time you quit. Don't make life harder for yourself. Quitting must mean that you do not smoke or vape, at all. Ever.

Nicotine withdrawal is a chemical process. You have no choice but to go through it if you want to be free. You must override your danger signals. If you can do this then you will free yourself from Nitch. This difficult time will pass. Be patient. It will take a while for the associations between nicotine and pleasure or relief to break down. But they will break down - as long as you do not take in any nicotine.

Cravings can be powerful but they also pass quickly. When one strikes, use distraction. Practice 'urge-surfing' using the skills you have learned through the Embracing Life script. Notice how you feel without making any attempt to get rid of the feelings. Just ride the waves of the craving and notice that if you can tough it out for a few minutes, the craving fades and disappears. Be wary of Nitch and his dirty tricks. He is dying but his propaganda machine may be very much alive. Watch out for Nitchisms and don't be fooled.

Relapse Prevention Downloads

2 self-hypnosis downloads dedicated to this are included.

Relapse Prevention Script

This is a script to help you prepare for high-risk situations. The recording helps you identify early warning signs and Nitchisms, as he tries to lure you back, and then to replace them with more positive and realistic thoughts, feelings and behaviours.

Coping ahead with likely challenges is a powerful way of improving your chances of navigating those situations successfully. Use this recording once you have made a firm decision to quit, so you can mentally rehearse the new positive and determined ways you intend to think and act as a nonsmoker. Repeat any time after quitting. This recording is particularly useful to use before you do the 'firsts' – first night out, first party, first social event with smoking friends etc. Use the specific situations in you will be facing in your visualisations, to help you mentally rehearse dealing positively and confidently with each scenario.

Thought stopping script

This script involves interrupting habitual responses to cravings and triggers, and interrupting your tendency to go into autopilot and reach for a smoke or vape.

The exercise is **SPOT IT, STOP IT and SWITCH!**

You need to SPOT the justification. Then STOP decisively, and SWITCH to a powerful short coping statement that resonates strongly with you.

Before listening to the script, it is important to develop some clarity about the thoughts and feelings you are likely to experience in those situations: the justification for smoking, the false reassurances you give yourself like:

> *It's not the right time to quit*
>
> *Just one won't hurt*
>
> *Come on, it's a party*
>
> *I've done really well, I can stop again tomorrow*

Develop a clear awareness of feelings that you experience in those situations: the cravings, the urges, the frustration, the sense of missing out, the agitation, the excitement as you sense yourself about to give yourself an excuse to smoke. Whatever it is for you.

You also need to develop some clear affirmations or coping statements to replace those feelings. When you are feeling at your most determined and committed, how do you think? What statements sum up that positivity and commitment for you?

Once you have your powerful coping statement(s), repeat it or them out loud, vigorously and with meaning:

You will NOT let Nitch hi-jack you. You WILL stay in control and make your OWN choices.

During this recording you will be asked to close your eyes and imagine the kind of situation where you are likely to experience cravings, urges, or triggers to use nicotine. You will be asked to verbalise these thoughts and excuses out loud, the way you might if you were at a party explaining to another person why it's ok for you to have one.

As you express these justifications when invited to by the recording, you will hear a loud STOP being shouted. This will jolt you from those chains of thoughts, and in the brief space the abrupt interruption creates, you are invited to visualise a bright neon sign flashing STOP and immediately SWITCH to your powerful coping statement.

The recording will invite you to take a deep breath and hold, and then relax as you exhale slowly, and repeat your coping statements in your mind, making each time more meaningful with more conviction.

This will be repeated, first with you verbalising the thoughts silently then shouting STOP out loud, and finally going through the whole scenario silently in your mind.

This script helps in high-risk situations, creating a barrier to just automatically reaching for a smoke, and instead allowing you to respond to urges, craving and high-risk situations more thoughtfully and constructively. Use this script anytime from quit date onwards, whenever you feel yourself wavering.

Key Concept

> Expect and accept cravings. They only last a few minutes.

Over time you will find that you are thinking about cigarettes or e-cigs less and less often. Cravings will become less intense and occur less frequently. Soon you will be going for several hours without thinking about it. Later still, you will start going for whole days without thinking about or craving nicotine. You are still likely, however, to have pangs in certain high-risk situations such as parties, holidays or times of particular stress.

A few weeks down the line, things will be much easier and you may rarely think about smoking or vaping at all. You may feel that it was very hard work, or you may feel surprised and delighted by how easy stopping was. You may now be feeling very confident that there is no way that you are ever going to be trapped again.

This can be a very dangerous time!

If you are sensible you will think, 'I am free. I will never start again.' But all too often people instead start thinking, 'I've cracked it. I'll never get hooked again. So I can just have the odd one!'

Key Concept

A high-risk time after quitting is when you feel free and are confident you will never get hooked again.

Just one puff

Nitch's propaganda machine is still waiting for the opportunity to persuade you to feed him again. Giving you a false sense of security is one way of doing that, letting you think that since you have stopped for a while, it is now safe for you to have the odd one here or there.

Most people who quit end up relapsing. This is especially true of people who 'dabble'. Even people who did not find it that hard to quit end up trapped again. When you go back to nicotine, which smoke do you blame? The first one you bought? The first one you had alone? The first one you had in the morning? No! It was simply the first one!

The quantity/frequency principle

That first puff feels safe because smoking or vaping are no longer particularly important to you. Imagine you quit eight weeks ago. The first few days of thinking constantly about it are a distant memory. Over the weeks, you found yourself thinking less and less about smoking. Whole days can go by without you thinking about it at all. You wake up in the morning and do not need to have nicotine. You are fine during the day at work. Most evenings are fine too. You feel relaxed and confident.

However, there are still occasions where the desire for a puff hits you again. Perhaps these occur when you are at a pub or a party, or when friends who are still hooked visit you. Having a puff on one of those occasions feels quite safe. After all, you barely even think about smoking or vaping any more, and just one won't hurt. Will it?

Yes! Because the only reason you are in the happy position of hardly ever missing nicotine, is that you have not had any.

As soon as you take nicotine in again, everything changes. Instead of being someone who has not had any nicotine for eight weeks, you are now someone who has had nicotine recently. You may feel a little concerned about that, and decide to stop again. A few days later you find yourself in a similar situation to the one in which you previously used. You tell yourself that you coped safely last time you were in this situation, so you can have another one. The frequency of smoking or vaping has gone from zero to one (i.e. you smoke or vape in that one situation only).

Once you are smoking or vaping in a particular situation (such as

Saturday night) the quantity of puffs in that situation also rises. Instead of having one, you may have four or five.

You then find yourself thinking about it and missing it in a second situation, similar to the first one. For example, Friday nights. Soon enough you have one on a Friday. The frequency goes up to two situations. Very quickly, having vapes or smokes on Fridays becomes acceptable in your mind, and the quantity on a Friday increases too. Now you may be taking in nicotine quite freely over the weekend.

As a result, you now find yourself thinking about smoking, or missing vapes on every occasion you go out. So you have the odd one during the week, when you are out socially. The frequency has gone up again. Once this new 'rule' for when you are allowed to use has developed, the quantity when out socially also increases. Now you may be smoking or vaping three or four nights a week. Once that happens, you start thinking about cigarettes or vapes and missing them every night.

Eventually you have a vape or cigarette one evening when you are relaxing at home. Soon you will be having nicotine every evening. And if you are having nicotine every evening, you will start thinking about it and missing it at lunchtimes. Have you spotted the pattern?

The more you vape, the more you want to vape. The less you vape, the less you want to vape. If you never smoke, the desire to smoke will eventually completely disappear, but if you smoke occasionally, the desire to smoke will increase.

The only way to be a non-smoker or non-vaper is to not smoke or vape. Ever!

> **Key Concept**
>
> The quantity/frequency principle says that situations you vape in, and the amount that you smoke in those situations increases over time.

Do not take it 'one day at a time'. Nicotine addiction is not a one-day-at-a-time kind of thing. In fact thinking realistically about the future can be powerfully motivating. Feeding Nitch is a lifelong chain that never weakens and never breaks unless you break it. The only way to break the chain is to accept that you cannot control it. You do not use nicotine because you want to, or you choose to, or you like to. You vape because you have to. It is not a free choice. One cigarette leads to the next and the next and the next and the next. The only way to break the chain is to stop smoking completely and permanently.

If you do relapse, it is very important that you do not give yourself false hope by telling yourself that smoking the odd one now and again will do you no harm. Instead you need to be honest with yourself. Remind yourself that nicotine addiction is not something that can be controlled. The only way to be free is not to smoke or vape. Ever. If you have slipped up you need to learn what you can from the lapse, restate your aim of never, ever, EVER…. and stop again immediately.

Learning from relapse

Many people have small slip-ups in the first few days and weeks of quitting. But just because it's common doesn't mean that it doesn't matter. Remember, 100% of people who relapse fully start with just one! If you have smoked one or two cigarettes in one or two places, do not kid yourself that this is fine. I'd love to be able to say, 'Well never mind, you've done really well anyway,' (even though you have), because unfortunately these small slips really do matter.

If you slip up there is an immediate impact on all three angles of the Nicotine Addiction Triangle:

- You re-awaken Nitch and reset the faulty danger signal.

- You fail to allow the conditioning to fade so you don't break the association between vapes and pleasures or benefits.

- You reawaken cognitive dissonance because you have the thoughts 'I'm quitting' and 'I'm smoking/vaping' at the same time. This in turn greatly increases your risk of believing Nitch's propaganda. So you strengthen psychological dependence too.

Don't make life harder for yourself!

The biggest problem you are likely to face is the newly reawakened cognitive dissonance. You will want to believe that it's okay, so you may say things like 'Just one won't hurt' or 'I'll only puff occasionally, and it won't really matter' or even 'I've done so well so I deserve a treat.'

Remember the classic scene in Friends when Chandler smokes again:

Phoebe says: *Oh, I can't believe you! You've been so good, for three years!*

Chandler replies: *And this - is my reward!*

A little further down the line, as it becomes obvious that the 'odd one here or there' is turning into the odd many here and everywhere, cognitive dissonance will get even stronger and you will start wanting to believe that you don't care that much about quitting anyway.

Instead of reducing cognitive dissonance by kidding yourself either that the slip doesn't matter, or that you are not that bothered about quitting anyway, you need an alternative way to reduce dissonance - and here it is:

Tell yourself that you made a mistake, which is fine, everyone makes mistakes at times. Tell yourself that the good thing about making mistakes is that you can learn from them. Tell yourself that the only time you will not learn from a mistake is by pretending it wasn't really a mistake after all. The little mistake was smoking or vaping. The huge mistake is pretending it does not matter. Remind yourself that you successfully quit up until the relapse so you have proved that you can do it. And most importantly, restate your objective firmly. Your goal is to not smoke or vape again. Ever!

Key Concept

If you relapse you need to work out why, correct it and stop again immediately.

Stress and relapse

When you were regularly feeding Nitch, anxiety increased between each cigarette or vape. Every time you fed him, this anxiety would disappear, making you feel a bit better. If life stressed you out, you had two problems:

1) The real problem in your life

2) The need to feed Nitch

Your overall stress levels were a combination of these two things. Your body could not tell the difference, since Nitch stress mimics ordinary stress. Nicotine use therefore reduces these overall stress levels, making you feel better. This is why people are more likely to smoke or vape when they are stressed, and why they believe cigarettes are helpful.

It is crucial to realise that they only feel helpful if you need the nicotine. Now that you are no longer a nicotine addict, smoking or vaping will no longer help reduce your overall stress levels. But it can be very difficult to remember this fact when you are in a crisis.

If you are nicotine free, any stress you experience will come from life, not from nicotine withdrawal. Therefore any solutions need to come from life too. But when you are in a crisis it is the most natural thing in the world to want to reach out for something to help you feel better. If you experience something terrible, such as a bereavement, unemployment or serious illness, you are likely to remember smoking or vaping as something that helped you cope. You are likely, therefore, to be tempted to start again. The trouble is that your memory is playing tricks on you. When you are anxious you remember vividly that in the past these feelings were relieved by smoking or vaping. **But only because your anxiety was caused by smoking or vaping.**

Think back to previous relapses. If you turned to nicotine at a time of crisis, what was that like for you? Many people don't even know, because they are in the middle of a crisis and have other things on their mind. But those people who can remember say the first cigarette did nothing at all to help. But having had the first, they had to have the second, and the third…

When I was in the middle of one of my many quit attempts, my husband was involved in a serious accident. I was waiting with friends at the hospital for news of his condition. My friend (who was a lifelong non-smoker) went to the shop and bought me some cigarettes. At a time like that, worrying about my own health seemed ridiculous, so I smoked them. I have no recollection of what the first two or three were like, but smoking is something that hooks you with extraordinary speed, so by the next morning I was re-hooked on cigarettes. My husband was fine, and I was a nicotine addict again. For the next week or so, while he recovered in hospital, I had to keep leaving his bedside to go down eighteen floors to stand outside in the snow to smoke. This was not helpful!

When you are stressed by life, cigarettes and vapes change nothing about the reality of your situation. You have to deal with whatever it is that life is throwing at you, whether or not you smoke. If you are a non-smoker, the real issues are the only issues, and smoking cannot help with those. Non-smokers do not think of turning to cigarettes to help them cope. There is no evidence that non-smokers cope less well, just because they are unable to use cigarettes as a crutch. In fact the research shows that non-smokers cope much better with problems, and are generally less stressed and happier than smokers.

One of the big concerns many health professionals have about vaping in young people is that they are so young when they start, that they have not yet developed robust problem-solving skills. From a very young age, they turn to a drug to manage life. There is emerging evidence that adolescents and young adults are increasingly struggling with resilience and poor coping, because they simply rely on drugs to cope, when it is far healthier and more effective to have your own reserves of resilience and strength to cope with the inevitable challenges of life and living.

As an ex-addict, the first cigarette or vape you have in a crisis will not make you feel any better. But unfortunately, you are likely to have memories that persuade you that it really does help. These memories are very powerful. The second smoke is also unlikely to help you, but very quickly your dependency reawakens, and you start to need nicotine again.

Within a few hours of your first lapse you are likely to be puffing away thinking, 'I really, really need these. I cannot possibly cope with this otherwise.' The tragedy is that if you had not had the first one, you would have coped just as well without any of them. But as soon as you reawaken the addiction, then you will need to Keep Nitch fed on top of all your other problems. If you are in a stressful situation, try telling yourself 'Thank goodness I've quit. At least my real problems are my only problems - in the old days I'd have needed to smoke or vape too.'

Beware false memories

Memories of how vapes or smokes helped you deal with crises are misleading because the memory is only one half of the story. People remember the relief, the 'aahh' factor, without recalling how stressed and miserable the need was in the first place. It is therefore crucial to fix firmly in your mind that cigs/e-cigs do not do anything to help with stress. Try to think of a time when you were desperate for a puff. Remember in as much detail as possible what that felt like. Then if you ever find yourself thinking about the 'aahh' factor, make yourself remember the stress of needing nicotine at the same time. You cannot have one without the other.

Key Concept

You can't have the 'aahh' factor without the 'aarrgghhh' factor!

A woman in one of my groups demonstrated this really well. When she first came to see me, she said she could not stop smoking because she had three children under the age of four, and the baby was ill a lot of the time. She therefore needed to spend many hours pacing up and down with the baby in her arms while he cried and cried. This was naturally extremely stressful and distressing. The woman felt that smoking helped her with those stresses. She described how she could feel the need to smoke getting stronger as she paced round the living room with her baby. She did not want to smoke over the baby, but leaving him made her feel guilty. So she would wait till the craving was overwhelming, then she would put the baby in his cot and dash outside for the fastest cigarette possible, before running back in to soothe her child again.

Others in the group could see that far from helping her, the need to smoke was an extra hassle that greatly increased her stress, but she was not able to see this herself at first. Eight weeks after quitting she came back to her follow-up appointment and reported how much simpler life was now that she no longer needed to smoke. Instead of three kids plus Nitch, she now just had the three kids to worry about. She was coping much better with her stresses than ever before.

Try to remember when you are stressed that being a nicotine addict is expensive, time-consuming and above all stressful. If you have problems in your life, the last thing you should do is add to them by waking Nitch up again.

Oops, I'm smoking/vaping again...

If you have a major relapse and recognise that you are addicted again, take heart! You can learn a lot from relapses, and this will help you when you quit again.

- Accept that you are addicted to nicotine again.

- Review how you were doing until you relapsed.

- Remind yourself of any positives that you discovered: for example, that withdrawal was not as bad as you had expected, or that you had stopped thinking about vapes or smokes a lot of the time.

- Write these down - once they have started again, many people forget that they were fine when they stopped.

- Work out what the triggers were.

- Identify any thinking errors that led to cravings or relapse.

- Create a plan for dealing with those triggers differently next time.

- Set another quit date.

A case example

Amy is twenty-eight years old. She stopped smoking by using patches for eight weeks. She did not deal with psychological dependence when she quit, so she thought of smoking as a pleasure that she was giving up for health reasons. She had awful withdrawal symptoms for about a week and then started to feel better. She avoided all social occasions for the first three weeks because she was scared she would smoke again. This made her fed up because she felt she would never really enjoy herself in the same way again. After that she began to go out and was pleasantly surprised by how well she coped with not smoking when she was out with her friends.

Eight weeks after Amy quit, her best friend, who was still a smoker, was turning thirty and Amy was dreading the party. She felt anxious about the high risk of smoking but felt deprived at the thought of going to the party and not smoking. She was certain she would have a miserable night and might ruin it for her friend.

She made the decision to smoke at the party. She told herself it was only for one night, that she had coped okay with not smoking, and it was such a special occasion that she would not risk ruining it.

She lit her first cigarette with excited anticipation. It was horrible. It tasted foul and it did not satisfy her. She was disappointed but tried another one. This one made her feel slightly sick. An hour later she lit up a third cigarette which was more like she remembered them. After that she smoked a few more, and was barely aware that she was smoking at all.

The next morning her clothes stank, her mouth tasted terrible, and she had no hesitation in saying, 'Yuck, never again.' However, that evening she experienced cravings again. She decided just to finish off the packet. There were twelve left. The first cigarette felt very satisfying. She smoked another before bed and smoked two a night over the next five nights.

The 6th evening was a weekend again and she was craving a cigarette. She did not smoke, but had a miserable evening. The next night she arranged to go out to the pub with some smoking friends and cadged a few of theirs. This pattern of occasional smoking at weekends or when out with friends, with a few miserable nights off cigarettes each week continued for another three weeks. Then one Sunday evening she was 'climbing the walls' as she thought about a whole week ahead of her before she 'was allowed' to smoke again. She went out that evening to buy a packet and accepted she was smoking again.

How could she learn from this?

Remember the plan:

Accept you are smoking:

Amy needs to acknowledge that she is back smoking again and needs to regroup for another quit attempt. She shouldn't try to stop again until she feels ready to set another quit date and give the attempt the thought and effort it deserves.

Review how you were doing until you relapsed:

Amy needs to be honest about what being a non-smoker was actually like, rather than focusing on what she expected or imagined it would be like. What she found was that withdrawal symptoms disappear quite quickly, that she was thinking less and less about smoking, and that evenings out were fine without smoking. What she also discovered was that she made negative predictions about what not smoking at a party would be like. These predictions made her feel deprived and miserable. Next time she should therefore concentrate on psychological dependence so that she can have a more positive view of life after smoking.

She discovered that the first cigarette was horrible, which confirms that cigarettes are not pleasurable in themselves - they just take away Nitch stress. She discovered that Nitch gets his claws into you again very quickly. She discovered that smoking was no big deal, in fact she can barely remember doing it most of the night. She discovered that even if you did not enjoy smoking, you will feel anxious and edgy a few hours after smoking, and this anxiety will lead you to crave cigarettes.

Remind yourself of any positives that you discovered:

Amy needs to focus on the positive things that she learned and write them down:

- I coped fine without smoking.

- Even going out was no problem.

- I overcame nicotine withdrawal without much difficulty.

- My imagination was worse than the reality.

Work out what the triggers were:

In Amy's case the trigger was a party. Or to be precise the trigger was a set of beliefs about the party, plus an inaccurate assumption that smoking just the odd one would not lead to full blown relapse.

Identify any thinking errors that led to cravings or relapse:

Amy needs to recognise that she tends to assume the worst,

even though she actually experienced that going out and not smoking was fine. She also falsely reassured herself that smoking occasionally would be okay.

Create a plan for dealing with triggers differently next time:

Amy needs to recall that the first two cigarettes were disgusting.

She needs to remind herself that she cannot smoke occasionally.

She needs to address psychological dependence so that she is not tricked by Nitch into misery and stress.

She needs to remember that she was fine as a non-smoker, even in high-risk situations.

Set another quit date:

And this time, deal with all three angles of the Nicotine Addiction Triangle.

Chapter Summary

- After quitting, expect and accept cravings.

- Cravings are just the faulty danger signal going off.

- Quitting involves overriding these danger signals.

- Quitting also involves breaking habits. Be patient!

- Nitch will be waiting in the wings hoping for a weak moment to snare you with propaganda.

- Not smoking or vaping means never smoking or vaping. Ever! All relapses start with just one.

- You will have memories of reducing your anxiety using vapes or cigarettes. It is crucial to remember that you only reduced Nitch stress, not stress in real life. Once Nitch is dead, nicotine cannot possibly help you.

- If you relapse, work out why, fix it and restate your objective immediately.

- This objective is (of course!) not smoking or vaping. Ever.

Chapter 14:
Social Smokers/Vapers and other smokers

By now I hope that the idea of being a so-called 'social smoker' or occasional vaper is less attractive to you than it might have been before you started reading. However, some people do desperately cling to the false hope of 'social smoking' and so it is important to explain exactly why this just does not and will not work.

The social nicotine user is this fabled creature who can 'take or leave' cigarettes/e-cigs, who only smokes and vapes on special occasions, never needs to, who can 'enjoy' a puff every so often, but is never out of control.

A person, in other words, who is choosing when, where and whether to smoke or vape, and who can go without with no problem. Therefore, they can enjoy all the pleasures of smoking and vaping, with none of the drawbacks. Sounds good? Well, let's take a closer look.

You may know people who are genuinely like this. You may also know people who present themselves and their behaviour like this, but are probably kidding you (and themselves).

Genuine 'social smokers'

Over 90% of teenagers who smoke four cigarettes will take up regular smoking. This makes nicotine one of the most addictive drugs on earth. However, not everyone does get hooked on nicotine as quickly as that. There is considerable individual variation in the ease with which a person can develop a dependency. Take alcohol for example. Most people can drink moderate amounts with no problem. Quite a lot of people can drink quite heavily without becoming alcoholics.

Unfortunately, some people are not so lucky, and do become alcoholics on smaller amounts of drink. The addictive processes for smoking are similar. Most people who use nicotine get hooked with frightening ease. But there are a tiny minority who can have a lot more and not develop a dependency. Even these people will get hooked if they take in enough, but they need to use nicotine quite a lot before this happens.

People who are lucky enough not to get hooked on nicotine (yet) have no idea what the behaviour is all about. You are not one of these people. It has nothing to do with willpower, skill, practice, superior character or finding the secret of how to smoke or vape socially. It is sheer chance. The social smokers themselves will not realise this and are likely to feel smug and superior. They may try to tell you how to do it. You can't. And nor would they be able to if they were born different. Ignore them. They do not know what they are talking about.

Key Concept

You cannot learn to control cigarettes. If you have ever struggled to control smoking in the past, you will not be able to control it in the future.

Misleading 'social smokers'

Of the social smokers/vapers you think you know, only a tiny, tiny minority are likely to be genuinely not hooked. The others think that they are in control, but are mistaken. Many social users are people who have been addicted in the past. Then they quit for some time. Then they started up again, but only small amounts at first. And that is the crucial point. People sometimes relapse with an almighty crash and are back on twenty, thirty or forty a day within a week or two of relapsing. However, some people ease more gradually back into the Nicotine Addiction Triangle.

But all are going in the same direction - back to regular nicotine use. Think back over your own quitting history, or the experiences of people you know. Smoking again after quitting starts with the odd one at a party or pub, then the odd few at the weekends, then the odd one on weekday evenings, then the odd few on weekday evenings, then the odd one at lunchtime and so on.

At each stage of this process the person may feel and believe that they are in control. After all, the smoker still remembers that they used to smoke within minutes of waking and it is nothing like that now, so they are obviously in control... aren't they ?

No!

The reality of all addictions is that the more you do, the more you need to do. In a step-by-step process, the number of different occasions or situations when you inhale nicotine increases, then the amount used in those situations increases, then the number of situations increases again and so on.

The reason people think they are in control is because they are smoking or vaping (and thinking about smoking or vaping) far less than they used to. But it doesn't stay like that. In all addictions the more you do the more you do. Social smokers are therefore just people who used to be regular smokers, and are on their way back to being regular smokers, while mistakenly assuming that things are different this time.

Key Concept

Some 'social smokers' are relapsing smokers who are on their way back to full-time smoking.

You never believed you were getting hooked the first time you got hooked, so perhaps it is not surprising that you do not realise you are getting hooked again. If you meet someone who assures you they are in control, wait six months. You will find they have either quit properly or is a regular user again. Social smokers also tend to underestimate how much they are actually smoking. Never believe what smokers tell you. Social smokers tend to smoke more than they think they do.

Self-controlled social smokers or vapers

The exceptions to the above rule are the people who want to smoke or vape more than a few each week, but do not allow themselves to. These people set themselves a limit and ruthlessly stick to it.

Perfect solution? Well no. This is a very difficult option.

Occasional users are still in the triangle:

- They keep Nitch alive (or they repeatedly resurrect him).

- They fail to break the associations between nicotine and social situations, work breaks, pleasure and relaxation.

- They keep psychological dependence going.

The result is that they think about smoking or vaping all the time. They live their whole life as if they were in the first week of a quit attempt - constantly thinking about it, experiencing withdrawal symptoms almost all day, and never being free. And there is no end in sight. They are still feeding Nitch, so Nitch will not die. But he is not being fed enough to satisfy him so it is like being permanently hungry. This is much harder than just quitting completely.

Key Concept

Controlling nicotine intake is much harder than total abstinence. It is like permanently being in the first week of a quit attempt.

Why aspire to this? In fact, why does anyone do it? Well, the answer, as ever, lies in beliefs and attitudes. People like this have extremely positive views of smoking or vaping. And the less nicotine they have, the more satisfying each puff feels, so the more powerful the fundamental misconception is.

The different experiences you have of cigarettes or vapes at different times is due to how hungry Nitch is at different times. Remember, cigarettes and vapes do not change. All that changes is your readiness to have one. If you are chain-smoking you do not want or need to smoke, so when you do smoke it is unpleasant. If you are smoking heavily but not chain-smoking, Nitch is less full, but is still not hungry, so a puff on a vape is meaningless, but not terrible.

But what if you have not had any nicotine for hours? Well, then Nitch is starving and the cigarette or vape feels great. It is at those times that you think, 'I can't live without these.' But the reality remains that the only reason it only felt so was so good was because before satisfying him, Nitch was making you feel so bad.

Ruthless self-control means people are experiencing Nitch misery almost all the time. When they finally allow themselves to feed him, it is such a relief. This relief is so powerful that it makes them feel completely unable even to think about giving up completely.

They cannot win. They will never be free, but they have to spend almost all day withdrawing from nicotine. This is not something to aspire to. Your best chance of future happiness and freedom is to accept that you will never take in nicotine again. Ever.

I know I can never smoke again. This is fine because - guess what - I do not ever want to smoke again. The secret of success, therefore, is to get yourself into a frame of mind where being a non-smoker is something you actively want.

What social smoking usually means

Often smoking socially is nothing more than an excuse to justify smoking. People who need to smoke, but do not like to admit this need to themselves, can kid themselves that they are 'just being sociable'. You may come across people who tell you in all sincerity that they only ever smoke a few when they are out - they in fact smoke a packet but then delete most of those cigarettes from their memory and wonder where on earth all their cigs have gone.

Other people go out every night of the week - to give themselves an excuse. The ability of people to delude themselves is hard to exaggerate. When I was studying for my degree, I transferred from one university to another and started at the second university in the second year. I lived alone, seventeen miles away from the campus, I did not know anyone, and everyone in my year knew each other already, so it was hard to make new friends. When I arrived at the university, I was ten weeks into another quit attempt, and feeling fairly positive about it.

One day soon after getting there, I went to the sports centre to see if I could join any clubs and get to know people that way. I saw a group of lads standing outside the centre having a cigarette. I stopped to have a chat about what they were doing, and they said they were climbers about to use the climbing wall and invited me to join them. I readily accepted. They offered me a cigarette. I accepted even more readily, telling myself I was just being sociable.

The next night I happened to find myself outside the sports centre at just the right time for the pre-climbing smoke and accepted another one, 'just to be sociable'. Now this was totally illogical. I had met them before and did not need to smoke to give myself an excuse to talk to them. I was, in any case, about to spend an hour climbing with them. But reality never gets in the way of a decent excuse to smoke! I spent the rest of the week smoking their cigarettes. Then I started buying my own. I still told myself I was just being sociable. After all, I only smoked with these particular people. It just so happened that I saw them every evening.

I started going on climbing trips at weekends and therefore smoked freely all day and all night when I was away. But I still did not consider myself a 'real' smoker and it was at least two months before I admitted to myself that I was a smoker again. Do not pretend you are only smoking to be sociable if the reality is that you are mostly being sociable to let yourself smoke.

Key Concept

> Don't kid yourself that you are only smoking to be sociable if in reality you are mostly being sociable to let yourself smoke.

Beware other addicts

A note on generational differences

My experiences of sabotaging smokers come from my own experience as a smoker, and as a quitter, on both sides of that coin – being persuaded to smoke, and persuading others myself. And from the many, many stories I have been told by smokers I have treated.

But in updating this book I have interviewed that younger generation of vapers: those who took it up in their teens and are now in their twenties and beginning to try to quit. They assure me that they never try to sabotage a quit attempt. That they fully support anyone who is trying to stop and would not share their vapes, even if asked to, let alone force vapes onto would-be-quitters.

Whether Generation-Z are just a kinder, more accepting and supportive group than we were, whether I happened to interview people who behave differently to those smokers I so vividly remember, or whether they are kidding themselves about their own behaviour, I could not say! If the following does not apply to you, that's fine. Be pleased you are supported and be supportive of others.

On the other hand, many readers are likely to be older smokers, like me, for whom the following is likely to remain relevant.

Sometimes addicts find it hard when other people stop. Recognise any of these?

- 'Go on, just have one!'

- 'Here, have one of mine - one won't hurt.'

- 'You deserve a treat.'

You may also find people offering you a 'friendly' invite to go outside for a smoke. Sometimes people will even light two cigarettes and hand one to you. If you smoke or vape you belong to a club that is very welcoming and being invited to share is hard to resist.

On ITV's X Factor in 2005 the presenter Kate Thornton was asked, 'William or Harry?' 'William,' she replied, before pausing. 'No, Harry – he smokes fags,' she declared.

So why are smokers and vapers so friendly to each other? And why are they particularly generous with their cigarettes and e-cigs to people who are trying to quit? The truth is that people feel insecure when other people quit. Remember the ostrich syndrome? People are terrified of the implications of their behaviour and try very hard to ignore, deny or distort these. One effective way of distorting reality is to believe in safety in numbers. If you surround yourself with other people doing the same things you are, it is easier to convince yourself that the behaviour cannot really be that bad. Can it?

This is just more of Nitch's propaganda. He will direct your attention to happy, smiling people using nicotine and say, 'if it really is so bad, why aren't these people more stressed about it? They don't seem to mind, so it must be all right really'.

The sense of solidarity among fellow addicts hides insecurity. People may not want you to quit, because this will highlight their own fears. They will try to make you feel jealous and will go on about how much they enjoy it, or how relaxed they are about their own behaviour. This is unlikely to be deliberate, but it can be devastating unless you are aware of it.

Never be envious of smokers or vapers. Remember the research - over 90% of people want to quit. If you do quit, they will almost certainly wish they felt they could too. No one takes it up with the intention of carrying on for life. Most people wish they had never started in the first place.

Dealing with other addicts

If people try to make you re-start, take a step back to work out why this is happening.

- Does the person feel awkward about being the only smoker or vaper and want you to help them feel less self-conscious? If so, this is their problem, not yours.

- Is your quitting making the person feel more anxious and insecure? Their problem, not yours.

- Does the person think that you will become a different person if you quit - and they like you the way you are? Prove to them that this will not happen. You will still be you, you just won't ever smoke or vape anymore.

- Is the person genuinely convinced you will be stressed and unrelaxed if you quit? Reassure them by what you say and how you behave that you are absolutely fine.

- Does the person need you to make them feel better about their own behaviour? Their problem, not yours.

- Does the person worry that you are going to lecture them and become sanctimonious and smug? Reassure them that you are not bothered by what other people do. You are not turning into a pro-quitting health bore by quitting, you are just quitting.

Miserable ex-addicts

People who quit years ago but still miss it can be very damaging to your confidence. Nitch will immediately latch onto this and tell you that the misery of quitting is not worth it. But what is really going on for these people?

The simple truth is that if people believed that smoking or vaping was wonderful the day they quit, they may well continue to believe the same thing years later. This is a tragedy, because people do not realise that they are missing a false memory. They miss the sense of satisfaction, while failing to remember how miserable the need made them feel first. They believe that they gave up something that gave them courage, comfort, confidence, concentration and creativity. Something that relaxed them and relieved them. Something that cheered them up when they were miserable, made good times even better, was a friend and constant companion. No wonder they miss it!

If nicotine really did all this, smokers and vapers would be more chilled out, relaxed, happy and contented than the rest of us. Research shows the precise opposite is true.

So why do so many people get it wrong?

Because the benefits are costs in disguise!

- Nicotine stresses you out, then takes some of that stress away.

- Nicotine distracts you, then gives some concentration back.

- Nicotine gets in the way of enjoyment, then lets you enjoy yourself again.

- Nicotine causes misery, then takes some of it away.

- Nicotine robs you of everything - courage, confidence, enjoyment, contentment - then pretends to be enhancing these qualities.

If you meet a miserable ex-addict, just remember that they are missing something that they never had. If you do not believe the propaganda, you will not miss it. On the contrary, you will be delighted finally to be free.

Chapter Summary

- Some people take longer to get hooked than others.

- Most 'social smokers' are really either relapsing smokers or self-controlled smokers.

- Most people cannot control nicotine intake at all.

- Even those who can control intake through will-power are never truly free, so this is a miserable and difficult option.

- The only way to be truly free is never to smoke or vape. Ever!

- People often find other people quitting quite threatening.

- People prefer 'safety in numbers' and may consciously or unconsciously undermine your quit attempts.

- Some ex-addicts still miss cigarettes or vapes. This is because they quit without freeing themselves from Nitch's propaganda.

- This won't happen to you, so don't let it worry you.

- Once you have freed yourself from Nitch both physically and mentally, nothing and no one will ever get in the way of your permanent freedom.

Chapter 15:
How to Quit

NOTE: If you have glanced through the front of the book and eagerly turned straight to this chapter, I am glad you are so keen, but please don't go any further till you have read the preceding chapters. You will not be able to follow these steps without reading and understanding the earlier part. Be patient!

Make sense of the book

If you can follow the logic of what you are reading, and can see how it applies to your smoking or vaping you are well on the way, even if you are still nervous of quitting. Re-read any relevant sections to make sure you understand before reading any further.

Challenge your thinking

Before you quit, listen out for 'Nitchisms' and challenge them. By 'Nitchisms' I mean the doubts and questions Nitch puts into your head. Review Chapters 6, 7 and 11 on propaganda, and try to catch yourself making thinking errors. Do not just accept what you think. Thoughts stem from beliefs and attitudes and may not be true. Question what you think, and if you notice errors correct them. Use the worksheets to help you:

- Identify your thoughts

- Identify the links between the thoughts and your uncomfortable feelings

- Develop alternative thoughts

Use the Motivation and Commitment download once you know how you would prefer to think and feel about nicotine addiction.

Make a clear commitment to quit

Your quit date is one of the most important days of your life. You will be making a huge decision that will profoundly affect your future health and happiness. Do not just drift into a quit date. Take some time to think seriously about your two alternative futures: the smoking one and the non-smoking one. Do the work-sheets at the end of this Chapter, and listen to the Motivation and Commitment script.

Life as a nicotine addict means living with Nitch. It means having to feed him whether you want to or not, no matter how inconvenient. It means experiencing the stress of nicotine withdrawal day in and day out. It means being controlled by the need to keep on taking in nicotine. It means having to think about nicotine, plan for nicotine and find ways of getting nicotine any time and everywhere. It means having to pay for this whether or not you can really afford it. It means living in fear of the consequences. And it means gradually worsening health, increased disease and a higher risk of premature death.

Life as a non-smoker/non-vaper means freedom from all that. It means no longer playing host to Nitch. Nicotine will simply not matter. You will not need to think about it, plan life around it, pay for it, and die for it.

Once you are ready to set your quit date you may opt to listen to the 2 Futures download. You may continue to smoke, but in your mind you have moved from choosing to planning. Alternatively, wait until you are actually quitting and play it for the first time the night before quit date and again on quit date. Then make a clear choice. Once you have made it, never doubt it. The 2 Futures recording will cement that choice deep in your mind.

Set a quit date

Once you have made the clear and committed decision to quit, then you move from planning a quit date to actually planning and setting one. Choose whether or not you want to use NRT, Bupropion or Varenicline. If so, choose which product and stock up. If you are using NRT, then you will quit on the day you start using the product. If you are using Bupropion or Varenicline, choose a day in the second week of the treatment.

Choose a day of the week that you feel will give you the best chance of success. Think about your smoking. Do you smoke more at work or at the weekend? When are the biggest danger periods likely to be? When you have chosen your date, make sure you stick to it. If you start allowing doubts to get the better of you at this early stage, you will struggle later on.

When you have your quit date, pay close attention to your thoughts and feelings, and use a journal to keep your thoughts clear.

Stock up on the items you want to help you quit

These might include sugar-free gum, lots of water to flush out your system, fruit and fruit juice to stave off constipation (a common symptom after quitting), and a notepad and pen for you to do the thoughts-feelings exercise described above if you find yourself struggling.

You can also use flavoured sweets in the same flavour as your vape liquid. For example, if you vape cherry flavoured liquid, buy some cherry flavoured sweets or tic-tacs. Lollies are ideal as it replaces the hand to mouth movement too.

Practice your relaxation techniques, meditations and hypnosis downloads.

The more skilled you become at these practices the more benefit you gain from them.

Smoke normally until you reach your quit date

When you want a cigarette, be conscious of what that feels like. Many people do not find the feeling of wanting a cigarette or vape unpleasant - because they know they are about to have one. When you want to use nicotine, imagine not being able to relieve that itch. The feeling then becomes uncomfortable. Say to yourself, 'this feeling of wanting a cigarette or e-cig is Nitch. Nitch makes me feel bad. Nicotine addiction is about living with these uncomfortable feelings, quitting is about being free of them.'

Become increasingly aware of the drive to smoke or vape. Remind yourself that this feeling is anxiety which triggers off a faulty danger signal. Picture taking in nicotine as resetting a faulty signal - which will go off at full volume next time it is triggered. Now picture ignoring the signal and letting it fade away and sputter out, like a flat battery.

Practise this visualisation regularly.

Stick to your quit date

Even if doubts persist, stick to your quit date. Many people find that their imagination is worse than the reality. Remember that if you are panicking, it is your thoughts that are making you panic - not the reality. Do not 'catastrophise' quitting.

The night before quit date

Smoke your last cigarette or puff on your last vape. You will have been smoking normally up to this point, so it should not feel 'special'. If it does, smoke 2 in a row noticing that there is no satisfaction or relief.

Listen to the 2 Futures download then immediately throw away all smoking-related materials such as ashtrays and lighters, vape liquid, spare pods, any dead vapes, any remaining cigarettes. If you find this incredibly anxiety-provoking it is important to question why. What thoughts and assumptions are giving rise to this anxiety?

If you still feel anxious and think that throwing cigarettes or bars away will make it harder for you to quit, then put them somewhere out of sight. At the end of the first week of quitting, when you have proved you don't need them, throw them away.

Some people like to keep cigarettes around to feel power and control over the cigarettes. This is fine. The problem is not so much keeping them, as the reasons for keeping them. If you feel strong and defiant, then keep them. But if you feel anxious and want them around 'just in case', then it is important to get rid of them before or very soon after quitting.

Quit with confidence

On quit date play the Two Futures, Motivation & Commitment and Relapse Prevention downloads. And any others you feel could help.

Banish doubt. Never question this decision. Think about how young children respond to different ways of saying 'no'. If parents say 'no' clearly and consistently, then toddlers accept it with little more than a murmur. If the parents mumble 'no, almost certainly not, not now anyway, well, we'll see….' then you will get no end of earache until you have given in. Nitch is the same. No must always mean **NO!!!** Whenever the thought pops into your mind, shout 'No' at yourself, then let it go. Use distraction. Force your mind onto something else. Do not argue with yourself. Just say, 'No.'

Save money

Create a money box and put it somewhere clearly visible. Each day put in what you would have spent on cigarettes or vapes. It is amazing how quickly the money builds up. Plan what you will do with your first £20, £50 and £100. Work out how quickly you'll reach these milestones with the worksheet at the end of this chapter.

Break down the conditioned response

If you have particular rituals or routines, change them. This only needs to be temporary but will help you get rid of the conditioned response quickly.

Challenge your thinking after quitting

Continue questioning your thinking and watching out for those thinking errors, like 'Just one won't hurt'. Beware 'accidentally on purpose' giving yourself reasons to lapse. Some people will engineer situations to give themselves an excuse. Be aware of this risk. If you find yourself scheming in this way, STOP!

Use the Thought Stopping script to help you.

Avoid danger at first

Avoid danger situations if necessary, at first, but remind yourself that this is temporary. It is important to realise that you are only giving up nicotine. You are not giving up everything else you enjoy. In time you will enjoy everything else as much as ever before. Start doing relaxing and sociable things as soon as possible, so that you prove to yourself that the links between these situations and nicotine fade. Use the Relapse Prevention download before you begin to go into moderate and high risk situations, so you can cope ahead with the challenges and deal with them confidently and positively.

As your confidence increases put yourself in more and more 'danger' situations. It is a good idea to avoid alcohol at first because drinking clouds your thinking and reduces your willpower.

Expect and accept cravings

When you experience cravings, think of them as Nitch. A craving is not a command, it is just a feeling. Let it be there. It will go away after a few minutes. At first the desire to feed Nitch will come frequently. Then gradually the cravings become less intense and the time between them gets longer. Picture the danger signal slowly running out of power until it fades away completely. Just like a dodgy television remote, you sometimes get a sputtering of life from something you thought was flat, but as long as you don't recharge it (by using nicotine) it will die in the end.

As your quit attempt continues, you will be moving closer and closer towards total freedom.

However, you may have a bad day after several good days. This does not mean that you are back to square one. Accept that progress will not be totally smooth, and hope for a better day the next day. Mindfulness of Breathing helps you learn to accept negative emotional states calmly. As soon as you do this they then fade away gently. Ironically, trying to block out negative emotion makes it last longer.

The meditations also help people get away from the 'what if' worries they can have when they are quitting, and helps them focus on the here and now.

Keep reading

Re-read relevant sections of this book. Use the chapter summaries to remind you of key points.

Use support

If you need extra support seek out expert help. You can contact me via www.aspirelifestyle.co.uk to book 1:1 support.

Keep busy

Plan activities not normally associated with smoking for the first few days, especially during evenings. Cinema trips, Netflix binge-watching sessions, bus tours, museums and galleries, spa visits, sporting activities, walks in nature, activity based socialising etc.

Congratulate yourself

You deserve it!

Worksheet

Get a piece of paper and a pen. Say out loud (and mean it!):

When I quit, I will never smoke or vape again.

Try to work out how you feel about that. Write down the feelings that come over you as you look at and say that statement.

Relief? Excitement? Terror?

Depression? Other?

Feelings

....

....

....

....

....

....

....

....

....

....

....

....

....

Once you know how you feel, try to understand why you feel that way. Write down the feeling and then write down all the thoughts you have that are making you feel that way.

For example:

Feeling: Anxiety.

Thoughts: How will I cope? Cigarettes have always been there for me.

Can you think of any counter-arguments to the above thoughts? Are you making any thinking errors? Which ones?

If your thoughts about never having nicotine again are positive, well done. You are on your way. Try to focus more on the positive thoughts than on the negative ones.

Use the following positive self-statements to get yourself into a more positive frame of mind:

- Quitting will give me confidence because I will have proved I can achieve challenges.

- Quitting will make me proud and give me the courage to attempt other challenges too.

- I never needed nicotine to cope before I started smoking or vaping. There is no reason why I need them to cope now.

- Being a nicotine addict makes me feel weak. When I quit I will feel stronger and more in control, and will cope better with other problems.

- Feeding Nitch is a hassle I don't need or want. I am looking forward to being free of the need to smoke or vape.

Add your own:

....
....
....
....
....
....
....
....
....
....
....
....
....
....
....
....
....
....
....

Worksheet

Kick-start your quit attempt with a dose of motivation. How much do cigarettes or vapes cost you?

per day

per week

per month

per year

per decade

What would you most like to do with:

£5

£25

£50

£100

£250

£500

How long would it take to save these amounts?

£5

£25

£50

£100

£250

£500

Congratulations Certificate

This is to certify that I,

....

am a non-smoker and non vaper!

Since quit date on ....

I have saved £ ....

I will continue to save

£ .... per month

Tick as Appropriate

☐ I am fitter

☐ I am healthier

☐ I am less breathless

☐ I look and feel younger

☐ My skin is rosier

☐ My senses of taste and smell have improved

☐ I no longer smell like an ashtray

☐ I feel more in control

☐ My breath is no longer bad

☐ My house smells clean and fresh

☐ I have more energy

☐ My family are proud of me

☐ I am very proud of myself!

Other benefits I have noticed

....

....

....

....

References

Preface References

1. Petersen, K., & Kinderman, P. (1998). *The role of positive beliefs about smoking in maintenance of smoking behaviour and relapse after cessation* (Doctoral thesis). University of Manchester.

2. Ivings, K., & Khardaji, S. (2007). Cognitive reframing of positive beliefs about smoking: A pilot study. *Behavioural & Cognitive Psychotherapy, 35*(1), 117–120

Chapter 2 References

1. NHS Digital. (2022). *Smoking, drinking and drug use among young people in England, 2021: Part 4 – Electronic cigarette use (vaping).* Retrieved from https://digital.nhs.uk/data-and-information/publications/statistical/smoking-drinking-and-drug-use-among-young-people-in-england/2021/part-4-electronic-cigarette-use-vaping

2. Chen, X., Yu, B., & Wang, Y. (2017). Initiation of electronic cigarette use by age among youth in the *U.S. American Journal of Preventive Medicine, 53*(3), 396–399.

3. University of Nevada, Reno. *What does vaping do to your brain?* Retrieved from https://onlinedegrees.unr.edu/blog/what-does-vaping-do-to-your-brain/#:~:text=Nicotine%20has%20a%20negative%20impact,which%20can%20cause%20brain%20damage.

4. Glasser, A.M., Johnson, A.L., Niaura, R.S., Abrams, D.B., Pearson, J.L., Villanti, A.C. (2022). **The health effects of electronic cigarette use in adolescents and young adults.** *The Lancet Public Health, 7*(5), e405–e414. https://doi.org/10.1016/S2468-2667(22)00040-8

5. Javed, S., Usmani, S., Sarfraz, Z., Sarfraz, A., Hanif, A., Firoz, A., Baig, R., Sharath, M., Walia, N., Chérrez-Ojeda, I., & Ahmed, S. (2022). A scoping review of vaping, e cigarettes and mental health impact: Depression and suicidality. *Journal of Community Hospital Internal Medicine Perspectives, 12*(3), 33–39

Chapter 3 References

1. Miller, W. R., & Rollnick, S. (1992). *Motivational interviewing: Preparing people to change.* New York & London: Guilford Press.

2. Lewis, C. S. (1942). *The screwtape letters.*

3. News Medical. (2023, February 23). *Study of adult e-cigarette users' attempts and experiences of quitting.* Retrieved from https://www.news-medical.net/news/20230223/Study-of-adult-e-cigarette-users-attempts-and-experiences-of-quitting.aspx

4. MedStar Health. *How to quit vaping.* Retrieved from https://www.medstarhealth.org/blog/vaping-quit-smoking

5. Moheimani, R., Bhetraratana, M., Peters, K., Yang, B., Yin, F., Gornbein, J., Araujo, J., & Middlekauff, H. (2017). Sympathomimetic effects of acute e-cigarette use: Role of nicotine and non nicotine constituents. *Journal of the American Heart Association, 6*(9), e006579. https://doi.org/10.1161/JAHA.117.006579

Chapter 4 References

1. Berlin, I., Singleton, E. G., Pedarriosse, A. M., Lancrenon, S., Rames, A., Aubin, H. J., & Niaura, R. (2003). The modified reasons for smoking scale factorial structure, gender effects and relationship with nicotine dependence and smoking cessation in French smokers. *Addiction, 98*(11), 1575–1583.

https://doi.org/10.1046/j.1360-0443.2003.00523.x

Chapter 5 References

1. Glantz, S., Barnes, D., Bero, L., Hanauer, P., & Slade, J. (1995). Looking through the keyhole at the tobacco industry: The Brown and Williamson documents. *Journal of the American Medical Association, 274*(3), 219–224.

2. Russell, M. A. H. (1990). The nicotine addiction trap: A 40 year sentence for four cigarettes. *British Journal of Addiction, 85*(3), 293–300.

3. Drug War Facts. *Addictive properties of nicotine.* Retrieved from http://www.drugwarfacts.org/cms/Addictive_Properties

Chapter 8 References

1. Robins, L. N., Davis, D. H., & Nurco, D. N. (1974). How permanent was Vietnam drug addiction? *American Journal of Public Health, 64*(12 Suppl), 38–43.

2. Silagy, C., Mant, D., Fowler, G., & Lodge, M. (1994). Meta analysis on efficacy of nicotine replacement therapies in smoking cessation. *Lancet, 343*(8890), 139–142.

3. Steinberg, M. B., Zimmermann, M. H., Delnevo, C. D., Lewis, M. J., Shukla, P., Coups, E. J., & Foulds, J. (2014). E cigarette versus nicotine inhaler: Comparing the perceptions and experiences of inhaled nicotine devices. *Journal of General Internal Medicine, 29*(11), 1444–1450. https://doi.org/10.1007/s11606-014-2889-7

4. Hellyer, P. (2024). Dual use of vapes and cigarettes. *British Dental Journal, 237,* 414.

Chapter 10 References

1. Silagy, C., Mant, D., Fowler, G., & Lodge, M. (1994). Meta analysis on efficacy of nicotine replacement therapies in smoking cessation. *Lancet, 343*(8890), 139–142.

2. Steinberg, M. B., Zimmermann, M. H., Delnevo, C. D., Lewis, M. J., Shukla, P., Coups, E. J., & Foulds, J. (2014). E cigarette versus nicotine inhaler: Comparing the perceptions and experiences of inhaled nicotine devices. *Journal of General Internal Medicine, 29*(11), 1444–1450. https://doi.org/10.1007/s11606-014-2889-7

3. Glantz, S. A., Nguyen, N., & Oliveira Da Silva, A. L. (2024). Population based disease odds for e cigarettes and dual use versus cigarettes. *NEJM Evidence, 3*(2), EVIDoa2300229. https://doi.org/10.1056/EVIDoa2300229